THE CLOSET BOOK

THE CLoSET BOOK

ELIN SCHOEN

PRINCIPAL PHOTOGRAPHY BY BRUCE WOLF

HARMONY BOOKS / NEW YORK

To my designing father, with love

Text copyright © 1982 by Elin Schoen.
Photographs by Bruce Wolf copyright © 1982 by Harmony Books.

Published by Harmony Books, a division of Crown Publishers, Inc., One Park Avenue, New York, New York 10016, and simultaneously in Canada by General Publishing Company Limited.

HARMONY BOOKS and colophon are trademarks of Crown Publishers, Inc.

Manufactured in the United States of America

Library of Congress Cataloging in Publication Data

Schoen, Elin.
    The closet book.

    Includes index.
    1. Storage in the home.   2. Clothes closets.
I. Wolf, Bruce.   II. Title.
TX309.S33   643'.1   81-23777
ISBN: 0-517-542854 (cloth)   AACR2
        0-517-545756 (paper)

10 9 8 7 6 5 4 3 2 1
First Edition

CONTENTS

ACKNOWLEDGMENTS

The Closet Book would not have been possible without Margo Asahina's energetic and intelligent research and organizational help and Bruce Wolf's fabulous photographs and moral support—not to mention the very creative efforts of the Harmony Books home team—Harriet Bell, Doug Abrams, Richard Layne, Esther Mitgang and Ken Sansone.

I am, of course, extremely grateful to every manufacturer whose products appear on these pages, as well as to every designer who contributed advice, references and ideas. In fact, it would take another book to list all the people I'm grateful to, but the following friends and contributors deserve special thanks: Charles Damga, Richard Lawrence, Jack Lawrence, Elliseva Sayers, Don Weiss, Don Constable, Eric Bernard, Michael Matinzi, Mario Lo Cicero, Dennis DiLorenzo, Selma Larson, Barbara Schwartz, Nancy McKeon, Edie Cohen, Bill Shoenfisch, Skippy Morrison, Tom McCavera, Helen Gurley Brown, David Brown, Sara Evans, Frank Vitolo, George Kovacs, Shirley Cohen, Anita Bayer, Gordon Parks, Midge Richardson, Ham Richardson, Dr. Penelope Russianoff, Leon Russianoff, Sandy Gibson, Vincent Tcholakian, Anahid Markarian and Oleg Chichilnitsky.

GETTING INTO THE CLOSET

All my life I have wanted to have great closets. Other people might dream of having the perfect kitchen (one in which you could manufacture your own line of soups if you so desired) or a quadraphonic sound system throughout the house. But I have always been into closets—in my head, at least. In real life, my closets have always fallen far short of the ideal—possibly because my ideal closet, until recently, was a good-size room in which I would meticulously hang, stack and stash a wardrobe that would someday be donated to the Metropolitan Museum.

In other words, until recently, I've thought of closets in two distinct categories: my own (an urban jumble), and walk-ins the size of an entire room. That there were many possibilities in between never occurred to me. If the Great Closet was out of the question, I figured, let the things in my closets fall as they may—I'd wait. Consequently, I never considered the potential of my existing closets. And, as it turned out, among all the other things they were full of was lots and lots of potential.

This is probably true of your closets, too. Even if you're not suffering from delusions of grand closets, as I was, you may still be ignoring your home's inner resources—its closets—simply because you never really took a good objective look inside them.

Entire rooms, of course, are left less than functional for years for this very reason. You move into a house or apartment. You paint the walls. You put furniture here and there. It looks nice—or even gorgeous. Every once in a while, you add a rug, a lamp, a painting. The room looks better—even spectacular. But you never stop to think how much more effective that room could be if it were partitioned with bookshelves, if the space under the window seats contained something besides air. For years, you've looked at the room's effect—not at the room itself.

So it is with closets. But with closets, it's worse. Let's face it, very few of us confront our closets openly. Closets, by their very nature, invite avoidance. As long as the rest of the living space looks presentable, what's inside the closets doesn't matter. Often, homes look presentable *because* the closets serve as dumping grounds for the rest of the living space. Or—the state of the closets reflects the state of the home: chaos.

Therefore, your closets are more important than you may think. In fact, it could be said that home improvement begins in the closets. If there is a mess behind those closed closet doors, there is also a message: more organized closets lead to a more organized environment, which leads to a more organized life. And, in nearly every closet (as in every life) there is room for improvement.

New York designer Eric Bernard's approach to rethinking space applies to closets as well as rooms. He always takes three things into consideration: space, budget and life-style. Most peoples' spaces and budgets are pretty tight these days. So it pays to make maximum use of even the tiniest closet—or, in case of a closet shortage, to discover nooks and crannies that can be converted to closet use.

As for life-style—let's put it this way: one man's pantry is another man's place for storing ski gear. Although logic must be applied in arranging a closet's contents, the contents themselves needn't fit the context of the room. I know of a woman who hangs all her clothes openly in the kitchen (giving the brick-walled room the aura of a Neopolitan streetscape) because she has no clothes closet per se.

Every-inch-counts planning is what really goes into the great closets of the world. A lot of other things can also go into them—baskets, bins, antimoth sachets—but the bottom line is brilliant use of space, wide open or not. And if it's not, you can make it that way through sheer cleverness.

"Sometimes I feel like I'm designing an airplane or a boat," Eric Bernard says of his experiences in many a less-than-palatial Manhattan apartment. In planes and boats, as in mobile homes and mom-and-pop stores, space is at a premium. The ways designers deal with our falling or floating or flying accommodations and the way shopkeepers just naturally man-

THE MULTIPURPOSE CLOSET Variety needn't mean clutter. Wines and wearables (as well as other miscellany) are neatly stored together. And the "fishbone" shelf arrangement is not merely for drama; it minimizes waste of between-shelf space. Design: Charles Damga

A LOFT ALOFT The principle of an airplane overhead luggage rack could be creatively applied to the space above a bathtub (page 93). Photo: Elin Schoen

APPLIED LOGIC *(opposite)* If your hall closet is where you hang your coats, then it makes sense to store your hats, outdoor boots, mufflers, tote bags, umbrellas and even some handbags and gloves there, too. Design: Skippy Morrison/Photo: Bruce Wolf

age to display tons of goods in hole-in-the-wall stores can make homes more efficient, too. *Display* is a key word—shoppers won't buy what they can't see. Likewise, in your home, you can't use what you can't find—and, therefore, forget about. Efficient storage means high visibility.

Consider the overhead luggage compartments of a 747 airplane. Now—think what you could do with all the wasted ceiling space in your closets and rooms.

The empty square footage under your sofas and beds can also serve as "closets."

Chairs and tables and room dividers can double as storage.

I may be stretching the definition of *closet* somewhat—but it is the concept of closet that should be pushed to its outer limits—not your closet doors.

Of course, organizing storage takes more than imagination. Closet shops in department stores—or the ever-growing number of closet boutiques—are the obvious source for products that divide space in order to multiply it. As living spaces shrink, the need for merchandise to make the most of them expands.

But beyond bona fide closet gear, you can be inspired by (or use) commercial display units and gadgets, some of which are as much at home in your closets as they are in boutiques. Yachting gear, from map-storage tubes (ideal for never-hung posters) to marine hooks, help make a shipshape closet. Certain office and school storage accouterments can put things in place at home, too. Perhaps the most fabulous closet development to date evolved from a device used, until recently, mainly in restaurant cloakrooms and in dry-cleaning establishments.

And the search for closet solutions can begin and end at your local hardware store—if you know what you're looking for.

Having great closets doesn't require a major investment of either time or money. I hope that my own quest for the ultimate closet—which also led to this book—gives you some insights into your own closets and how to make the most of them. My closets are still not perfect, by the way—except to me. But that's the idea. They work for me now. Next year, I may have a whole new set of closet needs.

Meanwhile, let's get to work on yours.

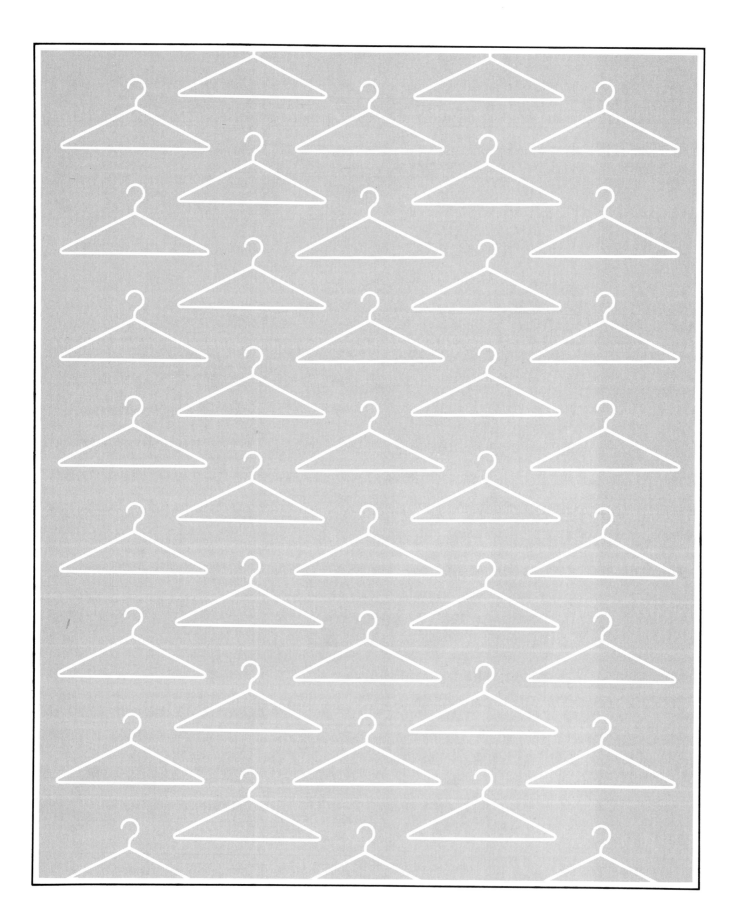

BEDROOMS

Bedroom closets, along with attics and basements, represent the deepest recesses of our life-styles. Closets elsewhere in the house tend to be better defined. There are broom closets and linen closets, cloak rooms and pantries. Bathroom closets are often extensions of medicine chests. Dining room closets hold dining gear. Closets, in other words, generally conform to the use of the space in their immediate vicinity. This makes them relatively single-purpose—and relatively easy to organize. And closets in public areas of a home are usually neater than the rest—because a visitor is just as likely to view the inside of a foyer closet as the foyer itself.

None of these things are true of bedroom closets. They are, in many homes, catchall spaces, likely to contain not only the clothes you wear regularly but your out-of-season garments, the spare pillows or the vacuum cleaner. Anything could, and usually does, turn up in a bedroom closet (assuming you can find it in the confusion).

But the main function of a bedroom closet is usually to hold your wardrobe—and maybe someone else's, too. And wardrobes are multifaceted. A clothes closet that really works, therefore, is one that is equipped to accommodate every sort of clothing as efficiently as possible.

Before deciding what goes where, and what system (homemade, prepackaged or purchased à la carte) best suits you and your possessions, you have to figure out how to maximize the use of the space you have.

1. Take everything out of the closet—absolutely *everything*, including those 400 fabric swatches from the time you reupholstered your chaise longue eight years ago.

2. Do your bit for charity. I know that with all that naked closet space spread out before you, it's a temptation to rush right in and decide what to do with it. But before you do, go through everything you've removed from the closet, item by

item. Throw out or donate to charity—it's tax deductible—the following:

- Clothes that have gone out of style and that you will never wear even when they make a comeback—such as the platform shoes that caused the fracture of your left ankle.

- Uncomfortable clothes—such as the handwoven Mexican wool shirt that gives you a rash around the collar area.

- Souvenir clothes—for instance, the loafers that never fit right but that you've hung onto anyway because you bought them during that unforgettably romantic weekend on Capri. If you really can't bear to part with such unwearable sentimentalia, find some other use for it. Turn a striking shoe into a planter. That Mexican wedding dress might do a lot for your wall, even though it never did much for you. Or you can just stash the sentimentalia—in another closet.

- Stained clothes—you've been meaning to dye that white shirt to match the wine stain on the breast pocket but never got around to it. Chances are you never will.

- Clothes that are totally inconsistent with your life-style. Let's face it, the chances of your wearing that orange blazer your brother-in-law gave you are nil. So why hang onto it?

- Clothes you've outgrown, physically or otherwise.

- Impractical handbags (likewise, briefcases, totes, etc.)—even if they were expensive.

- Entire categories of clothing that you never wear but feel you ought to have, just in case (of what?)—such as belts, hats, scarves, vests.

- Worn-out clothes—if fixing them would be more costly than they're worth, then so is hanging on to them, in terms of the space they take up.

3. Weed out nonwardrobe-related objects. Does the Cuisinnart really have to live in your bedroom closet? Are you sure you have no other place to store your place mat and linen napkin collections? If so, that's okay. Just plan to isolate nonwearables from wearables.

4. Take stock of your wardrobe, in detail. First, categorize your clothes according to season. Incidentally, gearing your wardrobe in the direction of clothes for all seasons makes closet

PRACTICAL CHIC *(opposite)* Partitioned, semicircular shelves on this closet door keep belts and bags in their place. The door shelves fit perfectly into the curved clear plastic shelves inside the closet when the door is shut. Design: Eric Bernard/Photo: Bruce Wolf

SHOE-IN Scarpiere consists of three- or four-door polyurethane units. Behind each door is space for six pairs of shoes—or more, if they are flats—each pair in its own ventilated cubicle. The units, which are available in white, black, green, champagne, blue and dark brown, can be placed side by side in your closet (or elsewhere). (Hastings Tile & Il Bagno Collection)

WELL-GROOMED ROOM The reason that this closet's capacity is so large is that its contents determine its configurations. Everything fits into its customized place. The distinguished gray doors slide to the side, accordion-style. Design: Eric Bernard/Photo: Bruce Wolf

planning—and life—a lot easier. Then categorize each season's clothes according to type. Don't stop with organizing the clothes themselves. Write down the results. That way, you'll be able to see, at a glance, how many blouses, skirts, shirts, and so on you have, and be able to judge how much space each type of clothing requires. Plan to store your out-of-season clothes out of the way. Now forget about your clothes for a while and take a look at your naked closet. You may have more space than you thought you had.

DOORS: A CASE FOR OPEN-AND-SHUT

Unless you don't need every bit of closet space, or access to it—but most of us do—sliding or folding doors are impractical. If the doors are the type that slide open within the door frame, one over the other, that means that only half of your closet interior is visible to you at any given time. If you have sliding doors that open into the closet, the wall space they cover when open is unavailable for shelves, rods or other storage gear. Doors that fold block a sizable part of the closet entrance when open and therefore partially obscure what's inside.

And the interiors of doors that fold or slide cannot be used for storage. So the space the door takes up, which can be invaluable when overall space is short, goes to waste.

Replace a space-consuming door with one that opens and shuts. If your closet's entrance is too wide for a single door on a hinge and your budget won't accommodate the construction work necessary to install a pair or trio of doors, try a curtain or blinds. Or simply leave the closet interior exposed. A beautifully organized closet in full view can enhance a room. (And the no-doors approach is an incentive to keeping it organized.)

FLOORS WERE MADE FOR WALKING

…even in closets. Loose items underfoot are not only messy-looking and possibly hazardous, they lead to "disappearing" possessions. The only floor space that should be used for storage is up against the wall. If clothes will be hanging over shoe caddies or boxes on the floor, allow for enough clearance space so that items on the floor are not obscured by the bottoms of dresses and pants.

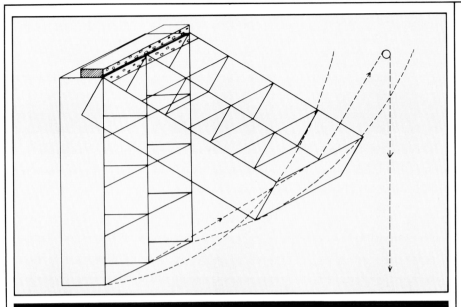

ROOM AT THE TOP

A big shortcoming in most closets is failure to take advantage of all the vertical space. Shelves or other storage fixtures can and should reach all the way to the ceiling. And even the ceiling can house sweaters, shoes, out-of-season clothes—anything that doesn't have to be hung up—with Scaletta.

SIZING THINGS UP

Now, take a look at your wardrobe again. The contents of your closet should determine its format—how much space is needed for each type of clothing, as well as what type of system best accommodates your clothes.

Measure your clothes, not only horizontally (ten shirts—not mashed together—take up about 8 inches of closet width) but vertically. In closets, as in airplanes, tall people need more room than short people.

Measure items to be placed on shelves. Someone with big feet will require broader shoe shelves, front to back, than someone whose feet are small.

Figure out how much space you really need for each category of clothing. Allow for some leftover space, especially if your overhaul is taking place in the summer (winter clothes are bulkier). And there's always the possibility that you'll add to your wardrobe—although generally the arrival of new clothes

SCALETTA Ladder, in Italian, is a compact "box" of shelves that fits flush against the ceiling. One end is hinged to the ceiling. On the other end is a pulley with which the shelves are lowered—for access—to stand vertically in what would ordinarily be unused space in midcloset. The concept is ideal for out-of-season clothes or items that would consume too much regular shelf space. Design: Oleg Chichilnitsky

DOOR-TO-DOOR SERVICE *(opposite)* This room has wall-to-wall built-in closets, each holding its own category of clothing. The open-and-shut doors do not interfere with visibility and access to the closets' interiors. Their screenlike construction keeps the closets' contents well aired, and also gives an airy quality to the room. Photo: Bruce Wolf

means the retirement of some old ones. In any case, the more "breathing room" clothes have, the better. I know a woman who irons everything she takes out of her closet before wearing it—but few of us are that fond of ironing.

SPLIT-LEVEL STORAGE

The multilevel hanging rod concept is the greatest thing to happen in closets since the invention of the hanger. The average closet contains a single rod, which is practical for long gowns, robes—anything that reaches almost to the floor. But all the space below the shorter clothes (which means most clothing!) is wasted. The basic multilevel hanging unit utilizes all that previously dead space, which allows room for more clothes and makes clothes easier to find.

You can install split-level hanging rods yourself (closet hardware is available in most hardware stores). Avoid tension rods. They may provide horizontal flexibility but they also fall down easily. Or you can hire a carpenter to do a fancier job, perhaps installing partitions separating the various-size hanging areas and shelves above low-lying rods for stacking sweaters, in the space beneath clothes suspended from the rod above.

THE INSIDE TRACK Attaching hanging rods to a track system enables you to raise or lower them easily by moving the brackets up or down a notch or more. Design: Eric Bernard/Photo: Bruce Wolf

DOUBLE SPACING *(opposite)* When you double your hanging rods, you double your closet's clothes-holding power. And the heights of the rods need not be permanent. Design: Eric Bernard/Photo: Bruce Wolf

TRIPLE SPACING *(opposite)* In addition to using double hanging, a large closet may be split in half with a partition that provides ample areas on either side to store ties and belts. Design: Sergio Mitnik/Photo: Bruce Wolf

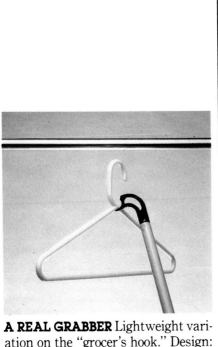

A REAL GRABBER Lightweight variation on the "grocer's hook." Design: Don Constable for Closet King/Photo: Bruce Wolf

OPEN-LEAF CLOTHES NOOK This particular leaf-through-your-wardrobe system is the Closet Spacesaver. It consists of metal wall tracks, wood bars that are attached horizontally to the tracks and have evenly spaced holes drilled on top and rods that plug into the holes and end in rubber-coated (therefore, slipproof) hangers. The hangers come customized to hold shirts, dresses, slacks and skirts. They pivot freely so you can flip through your clothes as you would the pages of a book. Design: Anita Bayer/Photo: Bruce Wolf

STORAGE-IN-THE-ROUND Long a fixture in dry-cleaning establishments and restaurant cloakrooms, the push-button rotating carousel for housing clothes has now been adopted—and adapted—for the home. The Automated Closet Carousel is made to order according to the closet's square footage and what, exactly, will go inside. The variety of options includes incorporating the Elfa Basket system (see page 128) into the carousel. The smallest revolving system requires at least 4½ by 7½ feet of closet space. Lacking that, some advocates of the system—which is surprisingly inexpensive—have had carousels installed right in the middle of their bedrooms. (White Machine Co., Inc.)

HIGH-WIRE ACTION Vinyl-coated wire systems provide not only split-level storage but the advantage of shelf space built onto the rods themselves and an environment for clothes in which air circulates freely. This system, complete with just-off-the-floor shoe rack, is Sani-Shelf by Schulte. The Closet Maid system (*not shown*) is nearly identical.

INSTANT DOUBLE SPACING The quickest and most economical way to expand hanging space is the Swinging Rod, which is suspended from the existing rod to provide another level. Its height is adjustable. Design: Don Constable for Closet King/Photo: Bruce Wolf

UNBEATABLE SYSTEMS

You can customize your closet's interior with any number of movable pieces that make up the system of your choice. The Stay-Neat system (not shown) operates on the same principle as Closet Spacesaver (see page 25). The difference is that the wall standards are oak, not metal.

IF THE SHOE FITS...

In closets, shoes have a way of getting underfoot. In a big closet, where shoes are not the only items stored on the floor, they also have a way of getting lost. Although this provides a nice element of surprise—it's always exciting to unearth your long-lost left Bass Weejun—your closet will work much better if you stop thinking of it as a big surprise package. Fortunately, shoes and boots seem to be top priorities with manufacturers of closet fittings.

OUT OF THE KITCHEN Metro Super Erecta Shelf system was originally used in restaurant kitchens and other commercial areas. It has since become the hallmark of the high-tech kitchen in homes coast-to-coast. But it also beautifully—and efficiently—accommodates clothes. It assembles easily and offers not only shelves with built-on hanging rods but all manner of storage options, including sliding trays, basket drawers that slide on under shelves and shelves with ledges to prevent things from falling. Systems can be wall-mounted or free-standing. (Metropolitan Wire Corporation)

SOFT SHOE STORAGE Hang up your shoes or sweaters in roomy bags with good visibility. Canvas sweater bag (*left*) comes in a variety of delectable colors, or see-through plastic bag houses shoes on sturdy cardboard shelves. Photo: Bruce Wolf

FOR THE WELL-HEELED An entire closet devoted to footwear provides both excellent visibility and meticulous organization. Notice the container of potpourri on the floor (but not underfoot). The atmosphere is further enhanced by a dehumidifying system located in the ceiling with the lights, which go on automatically when the door opens. Design: Richard Lawrence/Photo: Bruce Wolf

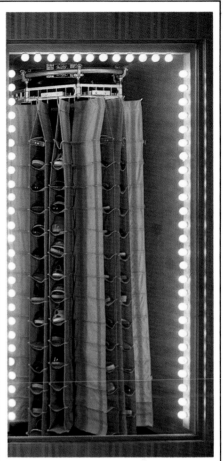

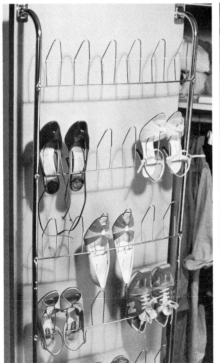

WALL POWER A boot solution that saves space and money. All you need is a pegboard (available at most hardware stores), the hooks that go with it and metal clamps with holes in their handles. Each pair of boots is clipped together with the clamps, then hung on the hooks from the pegboard. If there's no room for a pegboard on your closet wall, hang it on the door. Incidentally, pegboards are also useful for hanging up small handbags, beads and necklaces, hats, belts—and, elsewhere in the house, everything from kitchen utensils to gardening tools. Design: Skippy Morrison/Photo: Bruce Wolf

RACKING 'EM UP *(left)* Chrome-plated on-the-door shoe rack keeps 18 pairs of shoes in full view and in good shape. (Lee/Rowan) Photo:Oleg Chichilnitsky.

GIVE 'EM A WHIRL The push-button revolving shoe-bag carousel was meant for store displays. Still, if shoes are really your bag, it also makes sense on the home front. The smallest unit, which takes up about 4 by 7 feet of closet space, holds some 200 pairs of shoes. (White Machine Co., Inc.)

INSIDE STUFF: THE BEST BEDROOM CLOSET ACCESSORIES

The crux of any clothes closet is, of course, the poles on which you hang things. Closets meant for clothes generally come equipped with wood or metal rods. But changing the height of these built-ins requires major carpentry. If you're adding a pole or two—or starting a closet interior from scratch—use adjustable poles. One of the best rods around is by Knape & Vogt, nickel-finished and attached to the closet walls with slotted standards.

The best closet fixtures and fittings are the simplest. Closets should be designed, not decorated.

WHERE TO HANG YOUR HATS

Crushable hats can go in drawers or on shelves (packed in bins, baskets, boxes). Oversized hats, or hats that must be kept in shape, should be hung up—unless your closet has space for stacks of individual hat boxes.

HAT-CHECKING *(above)* A grid, and the hooks that go with it, is ideal for hats in or out of the closet. This one comes in basic black and white, as well as several primary colors. Photo: Charles Wiesehahn for Heller Designs

HOOKED *(right)* Garment hooks placed at intervals on the plain wood walls of this closet give it an old-time hat-rack aura and allow plenty of room for hats. Photo: Bruce Wolf

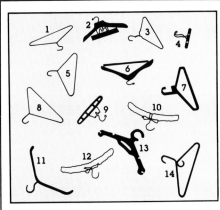

MAJOR HANG-UPS The only good thing about wire hangers from your dry cleaner is that they're free. Otherwise, the hangers shown here are better, much more supportive of your clothes.

1. Chrome-plated hanger (Bevco)

2. French Combination Hanger: a hardwood merger of French Collar coat hanger with trouser hanger (Lee/Rowan)

3. Lightweight golden aluminum hangers are rustproof (Goldbergs' Marine)

4. Slipproof trouser/skirt hanger opens by pressing the neck and closes by pressing the bars (Knape & Vogt)

5. Clear plastic hanger

6. Hardwood suit hanger with lock bar (Lee/Rowan)

7. Orange variation on the now classic tube hanger (Bloomingdale's)

8. Tortoise tube hanger (Bloomingdale's)

9. Jawbreaker, a snappy slipproof skirt or pants hanger (Lee/Rowan)

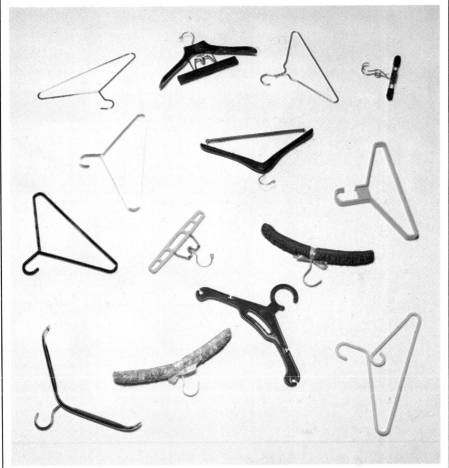

10. Model Home padded velvet hanger (Henry A. Enrich)

11. Chrome-plated coat hanger (Bevco)

12. Scented and padded hanger (Claire Burke)

13. The original plastic tubular hanger—designed by Marc Barnett in 1972 (Designworks, Ltd.)

14. Tubular hanger with hook for extra mileage (Bloomingdale's) Photo: Bruce Wolf

PACK-RACK Tubular steel folding luggage rack costs about a third as much as its department store counterparts and takes up scant space when folded. A closet luggage rack saves time: instead of dragging clothes out of the closet to pack, you simply move each item from its hanger right into the suitcase. (Bevco) Photo: Bruce Wolf

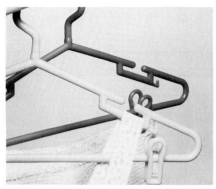

THE ULTIMATE HANGER Swiveler hanger rotates at the neck and includes notches with hooks and clips to make it truly all-purpose. (IPC Display Accessories)

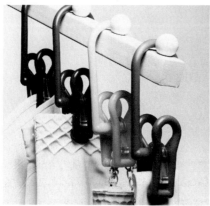

CLIP-ONS Hook Clip holds everything from umbrellas to ties to boots. (IPC Display Accessories)

HOOK-UPS IPC Clip can be used on pegboard hooks—or any hooks—in or out of the closet. (IPC Display Accessories)

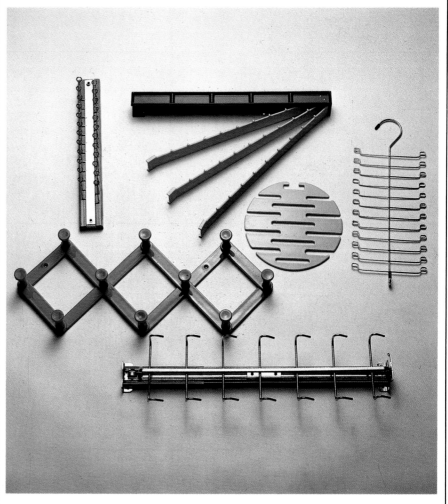

HANG 'EM HIGH Shown above are just a few of the hundreds of tie and belt racks.

1. Brass-plated automatic tie rack holds up to three dozen ties. (Lee/Rowan)

2. Plastic tie rack sticks to the wall with adhesive backing or with screws. It holds up to 30 ties on three swing-out rails. (Reston Lloyd, Ltd.)

3. Belt hanger attaches to wall with adhesive or screws and holds at least a dozen belts. (Reston Lloyd, Ltd.)

4. Wide tie and belt hanger goes right on the pole in your closet. (Lee/Rowan)

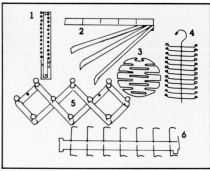

5. The Hooker is ideal for belts, necklaces or scarves. (Hammer Pac, Inc.)

6. Pan rack works for ties and belts, too. It pulls out for easy accessibility. (Knape & Vogt) Photo: Bruce Wolf

PURSE STASHING

Heavy handbags should not be hung up; it's too much of a strain on their straps. Plastic boxes (usually available in the hanger-and-garment-bag sections of dimestores) are not ideal for leather bags; leather has to "breathe." Open shelves or stacking baskets are the place for big bags. There are more options for little ones.

TIES AND BELTS

The idea is to see it all, at first glance, whether you put your accessories in drawers or hang them up.

Antique photographer's trays can also be placed on a shelf or in a large drawer to keep jewelry immediately visible and organized. Or order the modern version from Conran's.

NAILED A collection of antique purses hang from plain nails inside a closet. But the set-up would be both practical and decorative on the wall of a room, especially if closet space is tight. Design: Skippy Morrison/Photo: Bruce Wolf

TRAYED-IN Drawers can be custom-fitted with partitioned, sliding accessory trays. Design: Richard Lawrence/Construction: Joseph Teklits Woodcraft Corp./Photo: Bruce Wolf

GOOD SCENTS

Mothballs are not the only way to keep your closets moth free—which is fortunate, since few of us like to go around smelling like a musty attic. Two old-fashioned moth deterrents that smell much better than mothballs are dried rosemary flowers (put them in baskets or bowls on your closet's shelves) and a mixture of cinnamon and clove oils (place cotton balls moistened with the oils in muslin bags and stash or hang them in your closet).

SWEETS FOR THE SUITE Your closet needn't smell like mothballs to be mothproof. Shown here are some fragrant alternatives—as well as some plain good scents!

1. Perfumed papers for lining shelves or drawers (l'Herbier de Provence)

2. Porcelain pomander balls from Taylor of London and porcelain Penrhyndeudraeth pomander cat and elephant from Wales (Caswell-Massey)

3. Red-and-white cloth sachet with loop (Designers Guild)

4. Hanging closet sachets, picturesque and pungent, in lavender, Gentlemen's Scent, red rose, butterfly orchid, wild violet, lily of the valley and carnation (Caswell-Massey)

5. A trio of fabric antimoth sachets (l'Herbier de Provence)

6. The classic orange pomander ball—a Seville orange stuck with cloves and steeped in aromatic oils, then tied up with a gold cord for hanging (Caswell-Massey)

7. Tiny red-trimmed black hatbox stuffed with potpourri improves a closet's atmosphere. (l'Herbier de Provence)

8. Dried lavender blossoms in a porcelain bowl (l'Herbier de Provence)

9. Porcelain pomander balls (l'Herbier de Provence)

10. Cedar chips and lavender-scented cedar chips in porous bags (l'Herbier de Provence)

11. Pretty paper sachets made in Auckland, New Zealand—available with space for a greeting (Caswell-Massey)

DYNAMIC TRIO Three of the leading antimoth preparations are lavender-scented moth sachets (Reefer-Galler), chunks of pure camphor (Caswell-Massey) and cedar-scented closet spray (Reefer-Galler). Photo: Bruce Wolf

CLOSET ALTERNATIVES

Once upon a time, there weren't any closets. Clothes (among other things) were stored in pieces of furniture called armoires. Then there were wardrobes—armoires equipped with hanging rods. There are still armoires and wardrobes. There are also devices for turning walls into open-air closets. And quirky portable closets. And entire systems that turn walls into storage for just about everything, including beds and tables.

DECO-RATED Nouveau-Deco dresser-*cum*-wardrobe. Design and Photo: Charles Damga

TRADITIONS A traditional wardrobe in the Estoril Palacio Hotel, Estoril, Portugal. Photo: Elin Schoen

REVISING A CLASSIC This eighteenth-century French armoire held stereo equipment at one time. It is now a bar done in black laminate, mirror and glass. The whole interior is a separate piece that comes out in three sections—so there's no harm (such as nail holes) done to the armoire. Design: Richard Lawrence/ Photo: Bruce Wolf

CARPETED CYLINDER *(opposite)*
These are hollowed out for storage and rise from storage banquettes. Design and Photo: Charles Damga

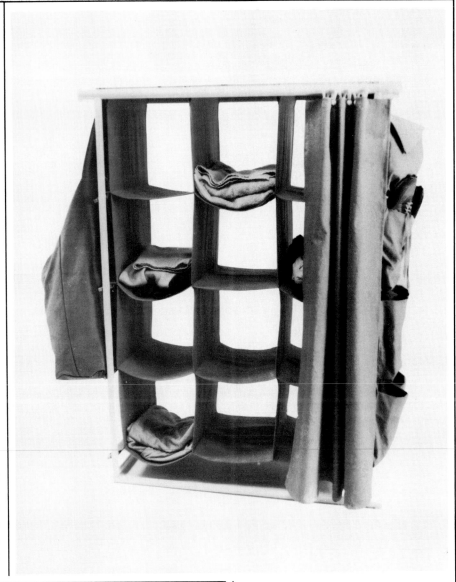

CANVASSING THE JOINT Soft Shelves consists of wood-and-steel-supported canvas compartments with a shoebag on one side, a laundry bag on the other side and a curtain to conceal the inside. (Up & Company)

CLOSETS TO GO

The one thing all the "closets" on the following pages have in common is that they're portable. They're much easier to take with you than regulation shelf systems or wardrobes—from room to room, home to home or town to town.

BE COLUMNED

Tall storage saves lateral space. High-tech designers have been using industrial cylinders for stylish storage for at least a decade. Charles Damga specifies all kinds of columns for caches with cachet.

THE AIR'S APPARENT The Unigrid System consists of interlocking lightweight mesh panels that are typically used to partition offices and rooms—but can also house clothes in a closet-less room. The advantage of open-air walls (aside from drama) is that clothes don't suffer from claustrophobia. (Beylerian)

PRACTICAL JOKE *(opposite)* The basic storage column with shelves inside is topped with a plant for a mock Corinthian effect. Design and Photo: Charles Damga

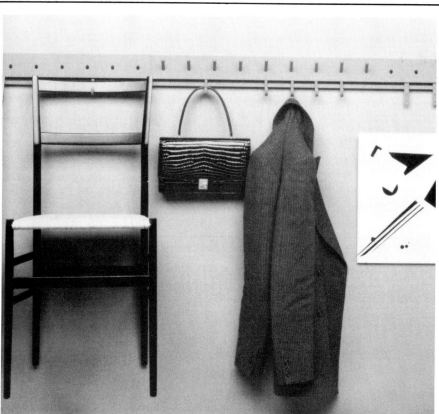

SHAKER MOVES The Shakers used to line their rooms with rows of wooden pegs, a neat idea adapted with the Outline System, which is made up of polystyrene pegs, wall supports, hooks, sliding hooks, baskets and shelves. (Beylerian)

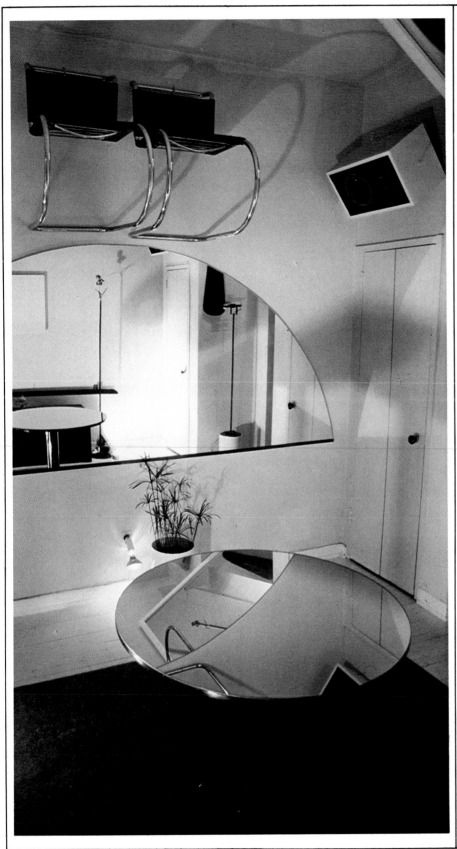

GIANT ECONOMY Two marine hooks is all it takes to accommodate spare chairs (or virtually anything else). This concept was inspired by the Shaker custom of hanging chairs on the wall. You can also use meat hooks, available from commercial kitchen supply houses. Design and Photo: Charles Damga

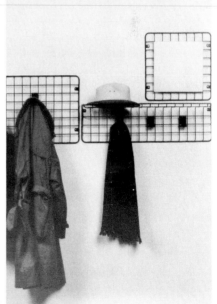

THE NITTY-GRIDDY The Graphis System offers wire grids in three shapes—rectangular, square and oblong (with shelf), along with flat hooks and wire hooks. (Beylerian)

REFLECTIVE ACTION Wall-spanning closets with mirrored doors. Design and Photo: Charles Damga

CAPITAL IDEA The storage column serves as the focal point for this studio apartment. Its capital, a simple shelf, expands storage space, as does the ceiling-skimming-plank connecting the column to the wall. Design and Photo: Charles Damga

THE FLYING CLOSET Simply a 32-inch-long wooden bar under a canvas canopy (good-looking as well as dust-catching). It hangs from the ceiling. Its height is adjustable. (Up & Company)

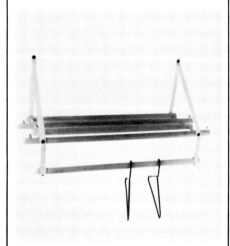

THE OFF-THE-WALL CLOSET A small wall unit (32 inches wide) combines shelf, hanging rod and wooden knobs for impromptu clothes-slinging. (Up & Company)

BEST-DRESSED CLOSET This palatial armoire is covered in the same fabric as the rest of the bedroom and contains plenty of hanging room as well as drawers, shelves and cubbyholes. Photo: Bruce Wolf

ALL IN THE WALL

A meticulously arranged closet system built in a closet-less room actually saves more space than it takes up—and not only because you can put more into such a system than into a wardrobe or into other individual pieces of furniture. When everything is behind closed doors, where there are no cluttered dresser-tops, the room looks larger. And you can expand the illusion of great space by mirroring the closet doors.

INTERLÜBKE This ingenious system is made-to-order in West Germany and consists of 22-inch- to 36-inch-wide lacquered wood cabinets containing hanging space, shelves, drawers, shoebins. Options include a home entertainment center housing television, stereo and speakers; a fully equipped bar; a swing-out work/dining table that seats five. Shown here is the revolving bed option, ideal for bed/living rooms—a cabinet-wall that swings around to reveal a pull-down bed. The cabinet-wall is also available with a double bed.

PHOTO FINISH With space at a premium these days, the Murphy bed is making a comeback. This photograph gallery doubles as a guest room. Design: Barbara Schwartz/ Photo: Norman McGrath

CREATE A CLOSET

Most rooms are full of dead space, and habit prevents most people from seeing the storage potential in them. When you're accustomed to your space looking a certain way, you tend to overlook the *really* exciting things that could happen in it!

TIRE PLACE The fireplace wasn't operative. Removing it would have been costly. It was camouflaged instead, creating a closet in the process. And the form, if not the function, of the fireplace is retained in the built-in aquarium. Design: Mario Lo Cicero and Dennis DiLorenzo/ Photo: Bruce Wolf

FIT TO SILL *(left)* The room had six cast-iron radiators under six windowsills. Richard Lawrence, realizing that two radiators would provide sufficient heat, replaced the other four radiators with "closets" housing stereo speakers and miscellany.

If there is no room under your windowsills to build *in* storage, you can always extend the windowsill and build the storage *out*. Photo: Bruce Wolf

MANTEL PIÈCE DE RÉSISTANCE Richard Lawrence could have simply hung a painting over this artificial fireplace. Instead, he built a television set into the wall and used a Cagli painting (with ¼-inch plywood backing the canvas) as the door. Inside the door is a signed Picasso lithograph. The whole arrangement saves space and triples the client's viewing pleasure. Photo: Bruce Wolf

WIRED A strand of nylon fishing wire suspended from the ceiling. The wire comes in various weights. This one is leather-jacket weight. Design and Photo: Bruce Wolf

NOW YOU SEE IT...NOW YOU DON'T Instead of leaving the space between chaise longue and window-wall vacant, a chaise-height storage system was designed to fill the spaces. Design and Photo: Charles Damga

ROOM AT THE BOTTOM (*opposite*)
People tend to stash things under their stairs. This procedure was formalized by enclosing the space under a winding stairway to make a closet in which cleaning gear is neatly stored. The walls are lined with easy-to-clean vinyl. Wood strips on the walls provide hanging space. There are special spaces for storing nails, tools and lightbulbs (which are arranged according to wattage!). Design: Richard Lawrence/Photo: Bruce Wolf

OVER THE STAIRS This "closet," installed via wheels to tracks on the wall, rolls forward when the owner pulls on a rope and fills the doorway to the cellar steps. When the steps, rather than the closet are needed, the closet is pushed back, well out of the way. Photo: Oleg Chichilnitsky

DOOR-TO-DOOR SERVICE Nowhere is it written that when you open the door to a room, it must go all the way to the wall. Yet most doors do. A door need not open wider than the doorway to which it is attached; the heretofore wasted area behind it is used as a linen closet. Design: Sergio Mitnik/Photo: Bruce Wolf

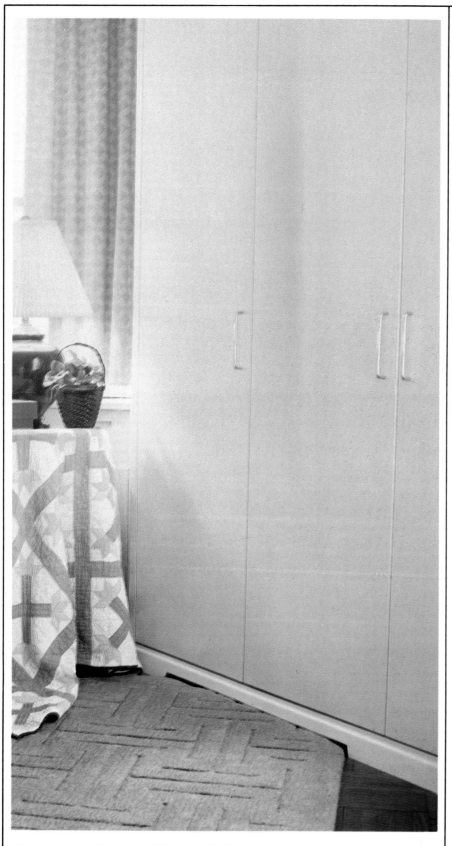

CORNERED A triangular closet was built to utilize some little used space. Notice how a hole was cut in the baseboard to accommodate an area rug. Photo: Bruce Wolf

WINING AND DESIGNING Where the kitchen joined the laundry room was a dead end. It has now come to life as a wine closet, temperature-controlled and complete with a glass door that is tinted to keep out light and that also "mirrors" the entire kitchen when it's closed. Design: Richard Lawrence/Photo: Bruce Wolf

CLOSET FURNITURE

Any piece of furniture that transcends its normal use by doing double duty as storage is closet furniture. It can be custom-made or manufactured—and more and more manufacturers seem to be operating on the theory that a chair should be more than something to sit on; a table should hold things elsewhere than on its surface; and so forth. In fact, the multipurpose room—the office/bedroom, bed/living room—that came into its own in the seventies has paved the way, in the eighties, for multipurpose furnishings. The notion is so intriguing that it's difficult to look at a plain chair or ottoman these days without regretting all the wasted space beneath or within it.

TABLES OF CONTENTS

How would you like to set your dining room table without commuting back and forth from the kitchen or sideboard? Having a place for place settings built under the table precludes all this legwork!

How would you like to watch television without having to make expeditions to the kitchen for snacks? The snacks are inside the coffee table right in front of you!

You can now find tables with room within for whatever you tend to put on top (not only place settings and munchies, but vases, decks of cards, tumblers, coasters, napkins, books, magazines, a mini-TV).

And closet-tables are not only convenient. There's nothing like uncluttered surfaces to enhance the look of a room (and give you a place to park your glass or prop your feet!).

UNDER-EASY The undershelf wire baskets that are currently showing up everywhere, expanding shelf space from kitchen to office, can slide beneath tables—or chairs and sofas, for that matter—to make them dual-purpose. These undershelf baskets are available in a variety of colors. (Heller Designs, Inc.) Photo: Charles Wiesehahn

SHELF-HELP This metal shelving is well placed so that it serves as storage for the study on one side as well as for the bedroom on the other. Design and Photo: Charles Damga

VANITY SQUARE The Ciarly Make-up Center is a dressing room unto itself, with fold-out mirror, swing-out trays and more storage space within the padded seat. (Hastings Tile & Il Bagno Collection)

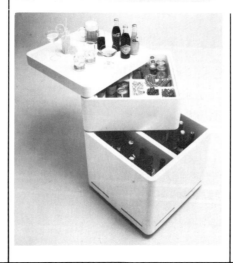

A MOVABLE FEAST The lower compartment of the Ciarly Bar is customized for bottles; the upper section is designed to hold everything from pretzel sticks to napkins. The tray on top means the whole piece does double duty as a table. (Hastings Tile & Il Bagno Collection)

HOT SEATS

Why waste space on a bench or chair that merely provides sitting room when you could have seating and storage in the same square footage? Some closet-chairs and closet-benches and closet-ottomans can be found in furniture stores (often literally ready to roll since they're on casters). Some can be custom-built (or built yourself). In any case, once you've lived with closet-seating, you won't believe you ever lived without it!

EASY REACH Shoes, ties, accessories are within easy access when stored in hinged platform seating. Design and Photo: Charles Damga

CARPETED MAGIC *(above and left)*
This two-tier seated arrangement is carpeted so that it seems to grow out of the floor. It contains, among many other things, a futon (Japanese folding mattress) that turns the tiers into a bed. Design and Photo: Charles Damga

BENCHED *(opposite)* The run-on wooden bench lining this living room is both sitting and storage space. Design and Photo: Charles Damga

CABINET SEATING Flip-top storage compartments with a removable mattress to sleep or sit on, a legless chair placed on top to underline the point: legs on chairs are redundant. You can't store anything in them. Design and Photo: Charles Damga

LOOKS AREN'T EVERYTHING This reproduction of the classic Mackintosh Willow Chair (the original was designed by Charles Rennie Mackintosh in 1904), has lots of room in its seat. (Atelier International)

TABLING THE ISSUE Stackable system consists of clean-cut tables—as many as you want—that get together, without hardware, to become a versatile storage unit that can partition a room (or go up against the wall). (Beylerian)

LONG DIVISION

Nearly every home or apartment has at least one multipurpose room—a living room/bedroom, a kitchen/dining room, an office/playroom. These rooms are not always physically divided into two or more parts. But if you do decide to divide your space, doing it with a storage unit makes infinite sense. You'll find that halving a room with a system of cubes or cubbyholes or shelves can nearly double its storage capacity.

TOP DRAWERS A basic storage unit from the Northridge System is assembled with a screwdriver. It can serve as a dresser, a nightstand, an end table or a highboy. It can also go under a table to make a desk. Multiple units can be stacked into a room divider (or wall storage) system. The canvas drawers come in many colors. The top is ponderosa pine wood. Design: Jerry Johnson for Landes

THAT'S ENTERTAINMENT *(opposite)* This elegant bar arrangement features storage space in its bases and room to lay out a buffet on top. The wine rack above doubles as a work of art. Design and Photo: Charles Damga

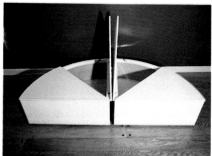

A WEDGE WITH AN EDGE The top of this pie-shaped hollow table is split to make two "doors" that lift open for access to the hollow interior. Design and Photo: Charles Damga

AT YOUR SERVICE

Some closet furniture virtually waits on you, keeping food and drink at your fingertips, keeping cosmetics in meticulous order. The pieces shown are among the most ingenious home furnishings in existence.

ON THE SLIDE Ash or walnut tables have surfaces that slide open for access to the storage area within. Design: Mario Bellini for Atelier International

PACKING IT IN Almost any old trunk makes a coffee table that doubles as a place to stash liquor, magazines, even out-of-season clothes. Photo: Oleg Chichilnitsky

TRICKS OF THE TRAYS Pivot-out round plastic trays stack up to a compact storage/serving utility in these rolling carts. (Beylerian)

TRUE GRIDS A glass-topped rolling grid cube hinged on one side for access to inner space (Beylerian)

A CAN FOR ALL REASONS Trash can/planter/container table (Beylerian)

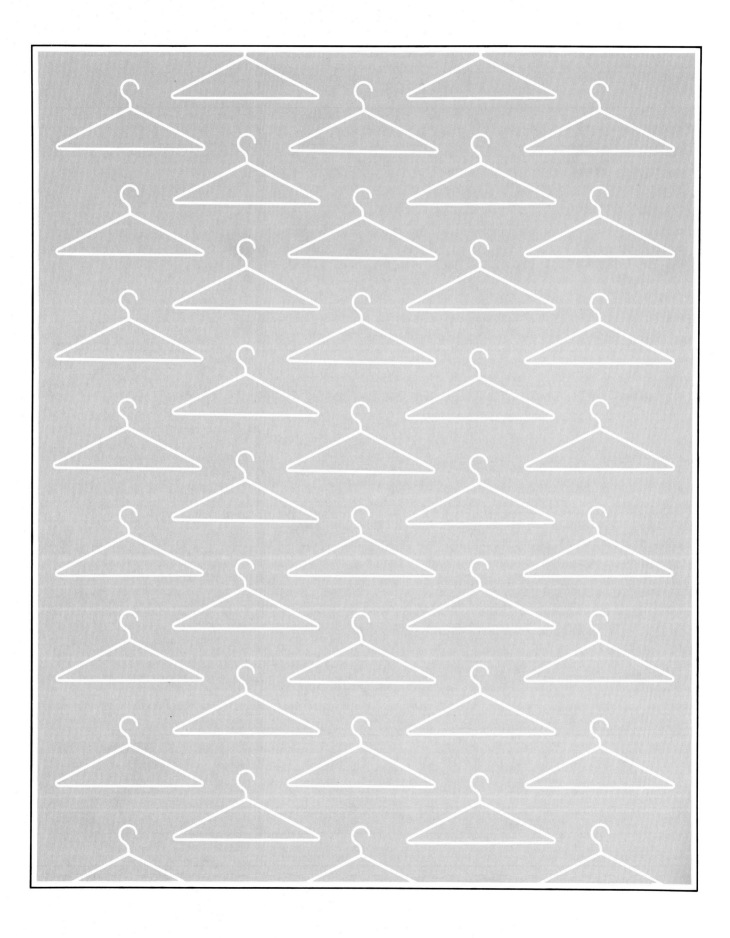

KITCHENS

Standard kitchen storage—the cabinet over the sink, the broom closet commodious enough for just that (a broom)—is pretty skimpy, particularly when you consider the great number of things that go into even the average kitchen. So the kitchen, more than any other room, is the place to wing it—that is, to really avail yourself of the space beyond any actual closets, all the *outer* space. Anything that can hang, should. Anything decorative can be stored in full view. The best way to get more out of existing closet space in the kitchen is to store as much outside the closets as possible.

Another key concept in kitchen storage is: what's up front counts. In other words, in and out of the closets, store items and implements that you use most often in the most accessible places. The salt, pepper, oil and vinegar, for instance, should be right at hand, along with the salad bowl, the favorite frying pan, the wok (if stir-frying is your mainstay) or the pasta machine (if you frequently do linguine yourself).

Anything you seldom use should be out of the way—but not so well concealed that you forget it's there. It would be a shame, for instance, to go out and buy a supply of expensive spices when you already have all of them buried in the nether regions of your pantry.

All kitchen storage should be geared to providing maximum visibility of food and the tools you need to prepare it. Partition and outfit your closets and cabinets to the hilt. Use walls, doors, windowsills, even the ceiling for hanging and stashing. The only places in the kitchen that are off-limits for storage are counter- and tabletops on which you work or eat. When allocating room for storage, never sacrifice the room you need to move things around on!

PANORAMIC PANTRIES

Most pantries, whether room-size or a matter of cabinets, feature big, deep shelves. These are very accommodating, but

not nearly as efficient as arrangements with many shallow shelves or shelves designed like oversize spice racks. With narrow shelvings, everything remains in sight and within easy reach—which not only precludes stocking up on items you already own but also prevents overcooking the omelet (or whatever) while rummaging through pantry jumble for a missing ingredient.

SPECIAL INTEREST CABINETRY

A good carpenter can work wonders in your kitchen, customizing your cabinets to hold specific items or building such accommodating cabinets from scratch. But this convenience comes ready-made, too—notably from manufacturers such as Mutschler and Poggenpohl. Cabinetry specially designed to hold wine, serving trays, utensils, linens—virtually anything that goes in a kitchen—is readily available.

WHEN THERE'S NO PLACE TO GO BUT UP *(opposite)* You can install a wall-to-wall shelf just under the ceiling to take the load off limited cabinet space. Design and Photo: Charles Damga

GOING BY THE BOARDS Never one to waste a millimeter, Richard Lawrence specified custom-cut crannies for custom-made cutting boards (juices drain into the sink when the boards are tipped over the lip of the sink) in the 4-inch-wide space where oven meets dishwasher. Design: Richard Lawrence/Construction: Joseph Teklits Woodcraft Corporation/Photo: Bruce Wolf

THE KNIFE BLOCK, which holds a better-than-average range of kitchen knives, is one of the many options available in kitchen cabinets. (Mutschler)

RIGHT ON POINT To accommodate the client's collection of kitchen knives, this slatted drawer was designed around 4 inches of dead space. The drawer is on full-extension, heavy-duty slides so it rolls in and out at the touch of a finger. Design: Richard Lawrence/Construction: Joseph Teklits Woodcraft Corporation/Photo: Bruce Wolf

A GOURMET DEAL Twenty feet of this kitchen wall were outfitted with a series of storage closets, custom-designed for the specific goods each holds. The closet on the right has shelves the width of one can, bottle or jar. The neighboring closet's shelves are twice that depth. And the owner categorizes his containers. For example, on a shelf of two-can width, if the front can is tomato soup, the can behind it is also tomato soup. Not all the closets hold food, however. There is a place for vases; one closet is all cookbooks. One door opens to reveal a stereo system. All interiors are polyurethaned for easy cleaning. Design: Richard Lawrence/ Construction: Joseph Teklits Wood-craft Corporation/Photo: Bruce Wolf

GOOD FOR SEASONING A swing-out spice rack triples this cabinet's capacity. (Mutschler)

IN-DEPTH STORAGE A wall's worth of foodstuffs is housed in several feet of kitchen space in the Chef's Pantry. Well-stocked doors open onto swing-out inner core of shelving. (Mutschler)

MAXIMIZE KITCHEN SPACE WITHOUT REBUILDING YOUR KITCHEN

A shelf here, a few hooks there, can vastly improve kitchen efficiency. There are dozens of products available for expanding storage capacity of your cabinet doors, closet doors, exposed or built-in shelves, even your kitchen walls and ceilings. And many of the products lend themselves to uses other than the ones shown here.

FOR YOUR PRESSING NEEDS The Iron-and-Ironing-Board Caddy uses almost no space itself, and it mounts easily on wall or door. (Grayline)

HANGERS-ON Slide-out cup rack accommodates a dozen cups, mugs or potholders. (Grayline)

UNDER-THE-SHELF Platter rack stows oversized trays or serving dishes in space that would otherwise go unused. (Grayline)

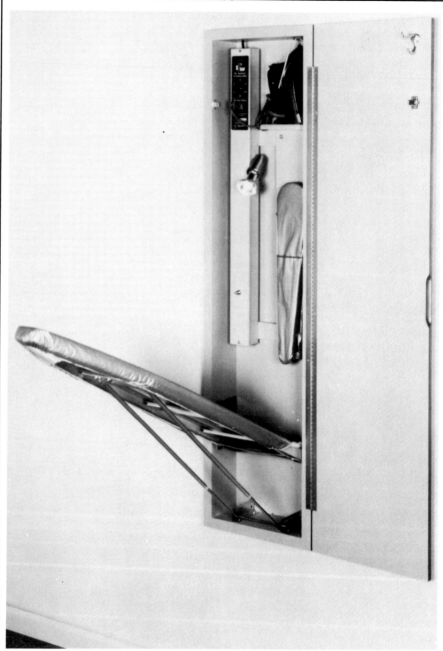

THE IRONING CENTER Fold-out ironing board, worklight fixture, automatic timer, appliance outlet, red indicator light and safety door switch, ironing board cover and pad and iron storage compartment are included. It can be built into your wall or surface-mounted. (Iron-A-Way, Inc.)

NOT JUST FOR THE BOOKS Revolving paperback display columns are available from newsstand suppliers. Vintage versions can be found in junk or antique stores. Photo: Sandy Gibson

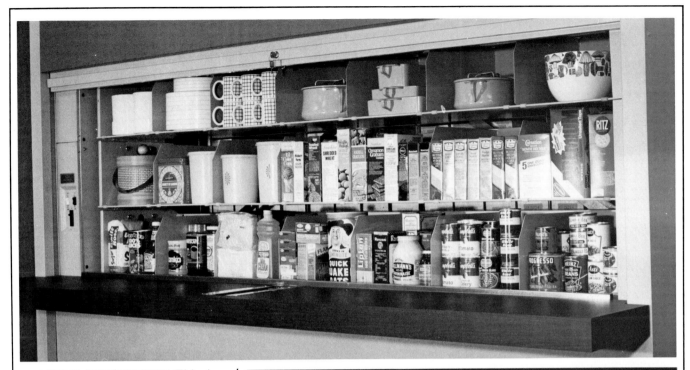

KITCHEN REVOLUTION This is a filing system commonly found in the offices of banks and multinational corporations. The levels of neatly partitioned shelving revolve vertically at the push of a button, bringing whatever you're looking for into full view. As White vice-president Donald J. Weiss proves in this picture, the system is a great boon to kitchens. It can extend all the way down to the floor below. It takes up 105 inches in width and 48 inches in depth. Shelf-arrangement options are numerous. And it costs no more than a kitchenful of quality cabinetwork. (White Machine Co., Inc.) Photo: Donald J. Weiss

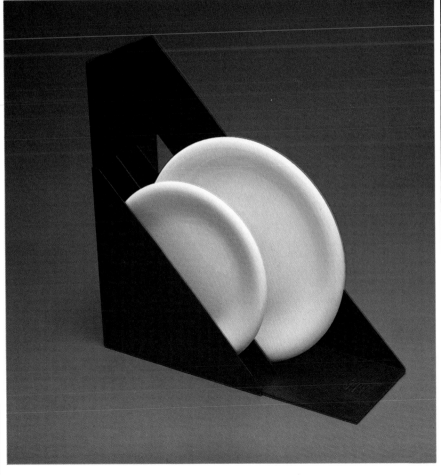

NOT JUST FOR THE RECORDS Plastic record album holders are great for housing cookie pans, oversize dishes, serving trays. (Heller Designs, Inc.) Photo: Bruce Wolf

BEHIND CLOSED DOORS Even the shallowest closet seems really deep with the Dor-Wall Rack. It could be attached to the outside of a door if it intrudes too much on a closet's interior. (Schulte Corporation)

WIRE WORKS Super Erecta Shelf systems, once found exclusively in commercial kitchens, have become as familiar on the home-kitchen front as wood cabinetry. Like a child's erector set, the shelves can be set up in an infinite variety of ways. (Metropolitan Wire Corporation)

SIMPLY GREAT *(opposite)* This is the best made-in-USA version of the venerable Italian slatted bottom shelf in an over-the-sink cabinet, which lets dishes dry without taking up counter space. If the unit is hung over the sink, dishes can be stored wet to drip dry. (Sun Glo Corporation) Photo: Bruce Wolf

BATHROOMS

You may not think there's *room* for improvement in your bathroom. Most bathrooms do not contain closets; they are closets themselves. But lack of either bona fide closets or square footage need not rule out efficiency—or drama.

First of all, treat the closet-less, closet-size bathroom as if it *was* a closet. Floor-to-ceiling shelves can hold everything from towels to cosmetics. Install shallow shelves on the bathroom door, from top to bottom.

If you like to store bathing items on the bathtub ledge (but hate when the bottles and jars slip from the ledge into your bathwater), extend the tub's storage capacity (and add a rustic touch) by building a wide plywood ledge around the rim of the tub. Polyurethane it or paint it. Your sink can be expanded the same way.

MAKING THE GRADES Gradated linen shelves were built so that each level is slightly wider than the one above it. That way, the overhead light, which goes on when the door is open, falls evenly on each shelf. The birchwood shelves are treated with polyurethane for easy cleaning and so that everything slides on and off the shelves more smoothly than a paint job would allow. Design: Richard Lawrence/Photo: Bruce Wolf

OVER-THE-SINK PRESCRIPTION

Allibert's modular furniture for the bathroom is made of laminated wood, inside and out. The components come à la carte to accommodate your needs. Cabinet interiors are partitioned for various purposes —for instance, a tall and narrow cabinet can come with hanging space and shelf or with shelves, drawers and a hamper.

Allibert medicine chests are unusually deep (4 to 6 inches) and have magnetic closing doors rather than the traditional sliding doors, making it easier to get at everything inside. Some doors have "balconies" inside for extra storage. All shelves and "balconies" are movable. Best of all, the chests contain childproof (or snoopproof) locking compartments. Options include: magnetic bar for scissors, tweezers, movable magnifying mirror, covered toothbrush holders, independent light system (with more than one outlet inside and space to store not only a razor but a hairdryer) and drawers.

HOT AND COLD RUNNING STOR-AGE The Lavandone is nearly 6 feet high but only 37⅜ inches wide and 22½ inches deep, so it fits into even a tiny bathroom. In addition to a deep basin equipped with a spray head, the Lavandone offers open linen compartments, a hamper, a spacious medicine cabinet, a radio and a neon light diffuser. The unit is made of polyurethane and comes in white, black, or brown. (Hastings Tile & Il Bagno Collection)

WHAT'S IN A WALL? Medicine chests are squeezed into this one—long, narrow spaces-with-shelves stashed between the support beams. The door panels are tiled to blend in with the rest of the wall. This system can be built into just about any wall, wherever there is no wiring. Design: Eric Bernard/Photo: Oleg Chichilnitsky

SHOWER POWER It occurred to Eric Bernard that the excess clearance over the bathtub was wasted space. This is true of nearly any bathtub or shower stall. Very few people need more than 7 feet of vertical space for bathing. Storage built into the area between the showerhead and the ceiling doesn't get in the way. Design: Eric Bernard/Photo: Bruce Wolf

A SMOOTH TAKE-OFF This shiny black laminate under-the-sink storage system is modeled on sinks in airplane lavatories. It slopes in from the top to allow standing room. Design: Mario Lo Cicero/Photo: Bruce Wolf

ALL THAT GLITTERS (opposite) The mirrored bathroom reflects the adjoining bedroom. The toilet and bidet are closeted. Behind every mirrored door is storage. Design: Eric Bernard/Photo: Bruce Wolf

FRESH ON THE WIRES Wire shelves don't warp, even in the dampest bathroom, and open shelving lets you know at a glance when you're short of towels. (Space Builder System by Closet Maid)

TOWER DE FORCE Pipedo, the revolving storage column designed by Carlo Urbinati, is nearly 7 feet high but takes up only about 1 square foot of floor space. On one side are shelves, drawers, a compartment with flip-down door and space for storing linens. The opposite side has shelves, a cupboard and a towel rack. Hooks for towels, robes, brushes, are on the third side. And the fourth side holds a full-length mirror. Furthermore, the shelves in the linen storage area can be replaced with a pull-out laundry basket. The unit comes in green, black, champagne, blue, white or dark brown. (Hastings Tile & Il Bagno Collection)

LINEN STORAGE

Towels of all sizes and washcloths should be stored in such a way that they are as instantly identifiable and as accessible as they are when hung side by side in a rack in the bathroom. And that's what the arrangements shown here accomplish.

TALL STORAGE

Columns organize the contents of any bathroom, but they're particularly useful in narrow quarters since they take up minimal horizontal space.

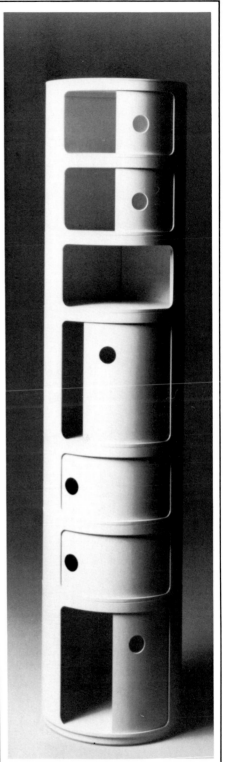

PITCH IT A combination roll-out garbage bin and clothing hamper under the bathroom vanity saves floor space. The garbage bin is easily removable. Design: Richard Lawrence/ Photo: Bruce Wolf

ROUND-UP You can stack these 16½-inch cylinders with slide-open doors as high as you want. The ceiling's the limit! (Beylerian)

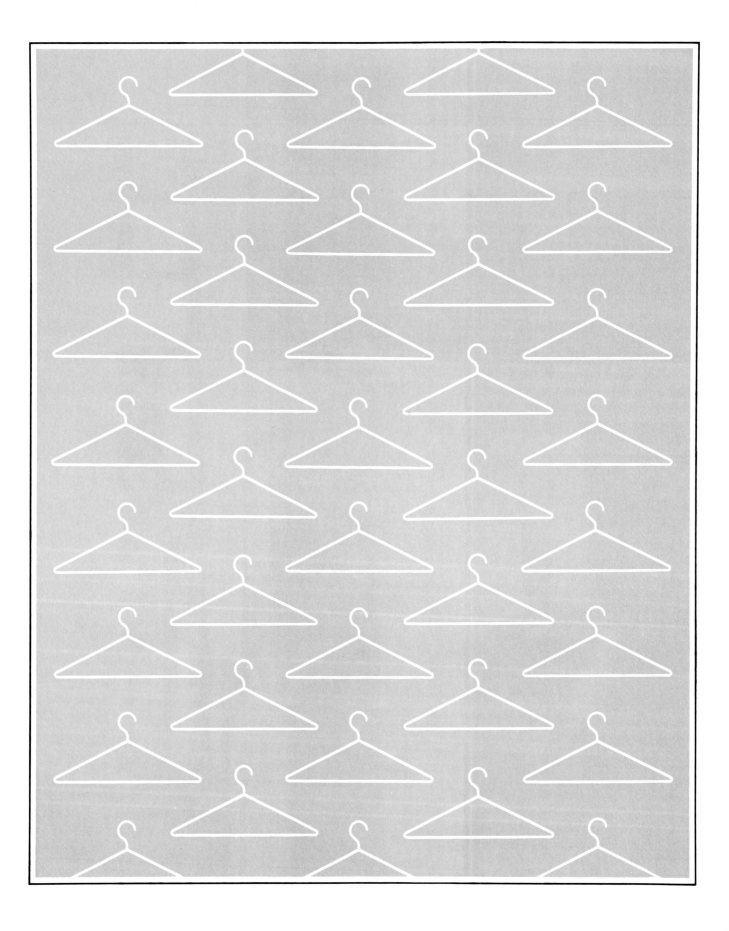

CLOSET ROOMS

Maybe you have a closet that is inconveniently located for conventional use. Maybe you have too many closets—and not enough other room. In any case, the conversion of closets into play/work areas (often, while they continue to function as storage places) is a growing trend. The closet room needn't be a walk-in. It can be a walk-up-to. The point is that the closet can come out into the open, revealing itself as another room.

WASH ROOM A washing machine and dryer fit perfectly into the closet in this child's room. Photo: Ricardo Salas Castillo

STRETCHING THE POINT (left)
Shaping up the inside of a tiny foyer closet is a Mach I weight machine. When the closet doors are open, the area becomes a gym. When the gym is not in use, the barbells, mat and bench fit inside the closet. Design: Eric Bernard and Michael Matinzi/ Photo: Ricardo Salas Castillo

COOKING CRANNY (opposite) This kitchen is one segment of a well-closeted wall. Small though it is, it's efficient. Contained in a space 3 feet wide, 2 feet deep and 8 feet high is a stove, refrigerator, sink and service for eight. Design: Dexter Designs/ Photo: Jaime Ardiles-Arce

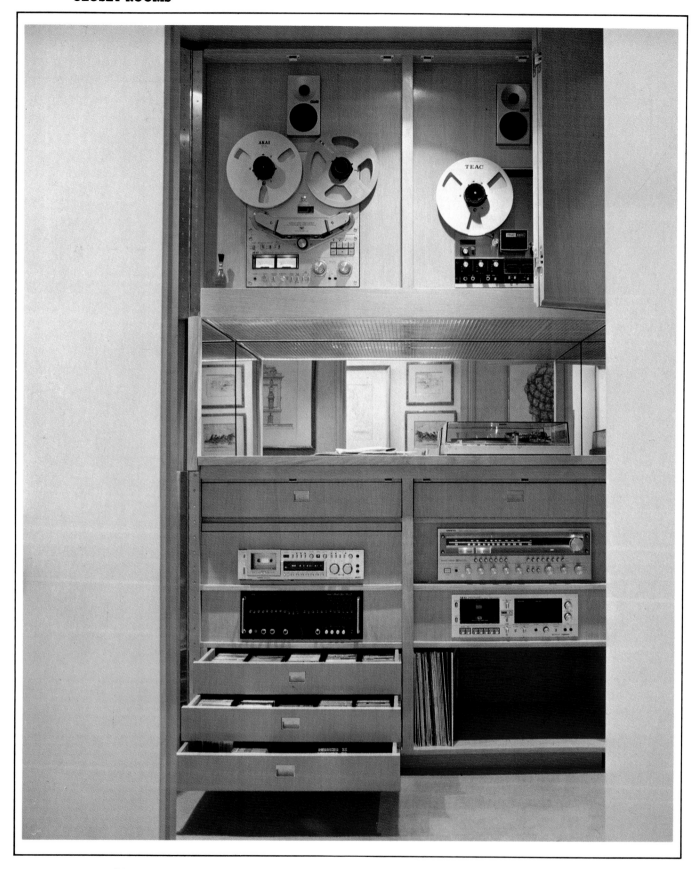

THE TURNED-ON CLOSET *(opposite and above)* Two long, narrow closets were turned into one and then the whole space was turned into a room for housing stereo equipment, with special drawers for filing the tapes. And the walls of the room became a record library with shelves rigged up to light up the labels. Design: Richard Lawrence/Photo: Bruce Wolf

HOT STUFF *(right)* In its former life, this electrically heated redwood sauna was a bedroom closet. Photo: Ricardo Salas Castillo

SOWING ROOM This closet, once occupied by a folding bed, is now an orchid farm, equipped with fluorescent lights, a humidifier and small fans to circulate the air. Design: David Madison/Photo: Edward Oleksak. Published with the permission of *House & Garden*, copyright 1979 by Conde Nast Publications, Inc.

DESK SET This home office system really works—as part of a closet wall or built in as a closet-in-itself. (Mutschler)

JUST WINE *(left)* Polyurethane foam gives a real *cave* look to this temperature-controlled wine cellar—formerly a bedroom closet. Photo: Ricardo Salas Castillo

WATERING CLOSET *(opposite)* There's plenty of storage space for glasses and what goes in them in this closet-bar. There is also room for a sink. And the mirrored walls and ceiling make the whole set-up look even spacier. Design: Eric Bernard/Photo: Bruce Wolf

CHILDREN'S ROOMS

Everything should be reachable. Everything should be adjustable. As the kids grow, so should the hanging rods, shelves, etc. (And flexible storage accouterments not only save you the time and energy it takes to redecorate; they save money.)

Safety comes first. Although locker systems (à la school gym), painted in cheerful colors, have come into vogue as a storage solution for children's rooms, they're only for children old enough not to get their fingers caught in the metal doors.

Allow room for fantasy. While it's terrific to organize your child's spaces as efficiently as your own (multiple hanging in closets, this space for heavy sweaters, that drawer for socks), there should be some free-for-all spaces, drawers or behind-door areas that can be as neat—or as messy—as the room's resident wants them to be.

And consult your kids, on what they want by way of storage. Their ingenuity may surprise you and it can be a big help.

BEDTIME STORAGE

Closetlike crannies under, on and around beds are made-to-order for children. The concept is more exciting than your average closet. And when toys and clothes are close at hand, they're more convenient to take out in the morning and put back before going to sleep—which can inspire kids to be tidier.

ROOM FOR ONE MORE When a child is old enough for a bed, simply remove one side of this crib. The drawer underneath can be used for storage, or when fitted with a mattress it becomes a trundle bed for overnight guests. (Lewis of London) Photo: Bruce Wolf

ROOM WITHIN THE ROOM There's closet space on either side of this child's environment. Note also that the shelf over the bed is padded, not merely to echo the organic form of the upholstery but to prevent bumped heads. Design: Barbara Schwartz/Photo: Norman McGrath

STEPPING-UP STORAGE (opposite) The space-saving, easy-to-get-into storage staircase leads to a sleeping loft, another space-saver, in a room that is only 6 feet wide. Design: Kenneth LaBarre and John Arakawa/ Photo: Bruce Wolf

THE SOFT TOUCH Bed Fellows is a versatile bunk-bed system complete with durable canvas accessories—pocketed guardrail and end-rail covers, pocketed saddlebag, bedspread, throw pillows, pockets for toys, books, clothes—anything. There are also under-the-bed drawers and a desk attachment. Design: Jerry Johnson for Landes's Northridge Collection

A LOFTY IDEA First, raise the bed, supporting it with a shelf-and-drawer set-up—and your child has a place to sleep, a secret play area and a storage space, all in no more area than the bed originally occupied. For maximum stability, attach the bed and/or storage/supports to the wall.

MAKE ROOM FOR BABY The Baby Block fulfills an infant's every need, with plenty of built-in drawers and shelves. And when the baby outgrows the crib, it converts into a child's bed. (Lewis of London) Photo: Bruce Wolf

STACKING UP Here are two staggering ideas for children's rooms. The plastic baskets are accessible—and mobile, if you take advantage of the casters option. The Storage Thing, already shown as perfect for bathrooms because of its minimal use of floor space, is ideal for kids' rooms because of its toylike appearance and easy-open sliding doors. (Beylerian)

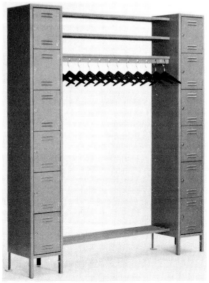

A CORKER It works in a child's room as well as in the classroom, where it is usually found. The corkboard with shelf-and-rod, plus shoe platform, takes up a 24-by-42-inch floor area and holds up to thirty-two items of clothing. A chalkboard can replace the corkboard. The height of both hanging rods and shelves is adjustable. (Claridge Products and Equipment, Inc.)

GYM-DANDY Kids of all ages love lockers. Among the companies that supply them in all heights and configurations are Able Steel Equipment Company, Adapto and Lyon Metal Products, Inc. The lockers shown are from Vogel Peterson.

FREESTANDING "CLOSETS" THAT ARE FUN TO LIVE WITH

Children are famous for their wonderful imaginations—and imagination is the key to successfully furnishing their rooms. But practicality is important, too. These two "closets" borrowed from school, battleship and gym, combine the elements of surprise and efficiency, fun and function.

BASKETS AND BINS

Easy access is a key storage concept for anyone—but for kids, it's crucial. Keeping their things within reach not only makes it easier for them to help themselves to the clothes and toys they want, but they'll be more likely to put the clothes and toys back where they belong. Your child's furnishings can encourage neatness as effectively as you can!

STOCK 'N' ROLL Boxes on casters are easy to get into and are especially good for stashing toys, since your child can pull them to wherever in the room (or house) he or she is playing. (NesTier Corporation)

SHORT STACK Stack plastic baskets with low-cut fronts so children of any age can get to each basket's contents easily. They come in a variety of strong colors. (Rubbermaid)

ACCESSORIES

What covers the walls and floors of a closet is a matter of personal preference, of course. I've seen lots of closets covered in floral prints and Scottish plaids, with storage boxes and garment bags to match. One memorable closet was lacquered fire-engine red inside and out. My own preference is for neutral color paint, since I feel that the closet's contents, not its contours, should stand out. And, while some designers insist on carpeted floors in closets—and I agree that if a room is carpeted, continuing the carpeting into the closet is a nice touch—I prefer tiled or wood floors.

There are, however, some specific principles of closet planning, suggested by expert Richard Lawrence.

1. Leave enough space between the surface of the floor (carpeted or otherwise) and the bottom of the door to allow adequate ventilation—as a safety measure.

2. Unless there are small children around, a doorknob is necessary only outside the closet; inside, a turn-latch will do. Most people don't go inside a closet and close the door behind them. Two doorknobs are an extravagance.

3. Even *one* doorknob is an extravagance when you consider the fact that handsome wire pulls cost less than $2.00 at most hardware stores. With heavy-duty magnetic catches, wire offers a simple, attractive means of opening and shutting closet doors. (This is, by the way, a guiding principle of kitchen cabinetry translated into larger terms.)

4. For easy-to-clean luxury, laminate wallcoverings are super-washable and handsome (for example, the Design Concepts series by Formica comes in subtle colors, graph-patterns and pinstripes). Vinyl wall coverings are not only washable but also fireproof.

5. A simple matter of esthetics: merely having uniform hangers in a closet—rather than some wood, some yellow plastic, some green plastic—makes for a more organized and attractive look.

HIDE AND SEEK The Closet Vault hides on a closet shelf to protect your valuables from fire or theft. The Wall Vault is even safer if it's built into a closet wall (as opposed to one outside the closet). (Meilink)

HANGING IN THERE Hooks can straighten out a closet's interior, or they can turn part, or all, of a wall into a closet.

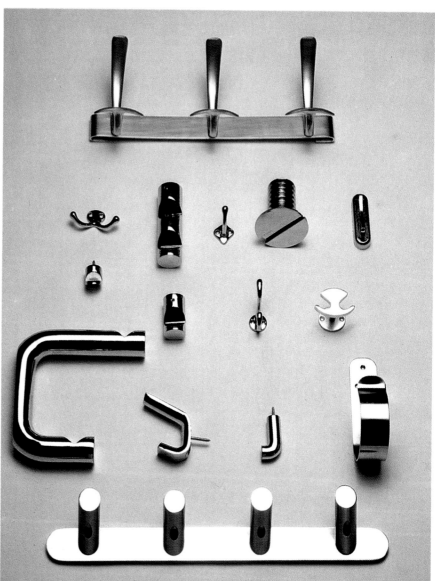

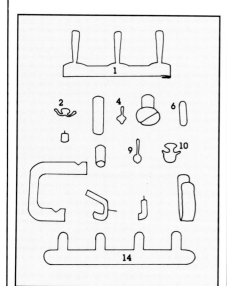

1. Garment rack (Peter Pepper Products, Inc.)

2, 4, 9. Wardrobe hooks (Goldbergs' Marine)

6. Aluminum fold-down garment hooks (Goldbergs' Marine)

10. Triple-duty hook (Peter Pepper Products, Inc.)

14. Large aluminum hook (Goldbergs' Marine) All other hooks shown are polished chrome Wall Customers. (Architectural Supplements, Inc.) Photo: Bruce Wolf

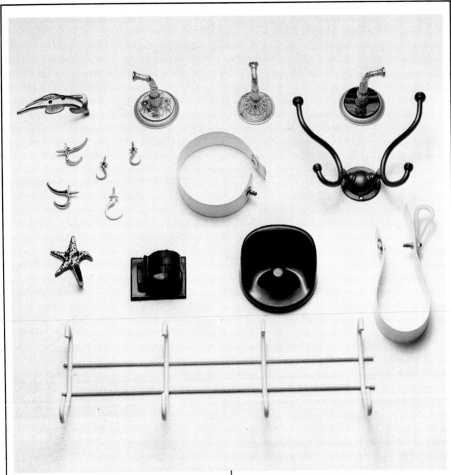

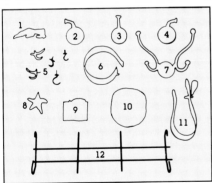

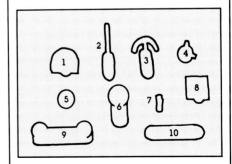

5. Assorted hooks from the dimestore, each under 50 cents, can be lined up on a closet wall for belts, ties, costume jewelry. (Gries Reproducer Company)

6, 11. White plastic marine rope loops, good for scarves, handbags, belts, beads (Goldbergs' Marine)

7. Antique brass garment hook

8. Brass Starfish hook (Goldbergs' Marine)

9. Brown plastic rope loop (Goldbergs' Marine)

10. Olaf coat hook (Beylerian)

12. Eight-prong All Purpose Rack (Closet Maid Corporation)
Photo: Bruce Wolf

1. Brass shark-shaped hook (Goldbergs' Marine)

2, 3, 4. Summer garden design with gold plate, all gold plate and malachite insert with gold plate (Sherle Wagner)

These hooks and knobs available in white, yellow, red, brown, blue and sometimes chrome.

1. Jumbo Hook

2, 3. Clothes Rods

4. Triple Ceiling Swivel Hook

5. Everything Ceiling Hook

6. Clothes Knob

7. Mono Hook

8. Sky Hook

9. Hang 2 (IDG)

10. Hook by 4

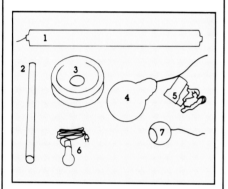

ILLUMINATING IDEAS Some designers specify incandescent lighting for closets because it is more natural; others prefer economizing with fluorescents. The selection here includes both.

1. Supertube, available in a variety of colors, can be used individually or lined up side by side for a lit-up pipe effect. The slim fixture uses little space or electricity. (It takes a 20-watt fluorescent bulb.) Design: Anders Peterson for George Kovacs

2. "Britestick" sticks to the wall, without fixtures. (General Electric)

3. Fluorescent coils require little ceiling space. (General Electric)

4. The Thomas A. Edison light, designed by Ingo Maurer in honor of the inventor's hundredth birthday (George Kovacs)

5. Passat 63 clips onto a shelf or hanging rod for spotlighting. (George Kovacs)

MAKING LIGHT OF THINGS

If your single lightbulb (the usual closet lighting arrangement) illuminates only part of the closet, install a more far-reaching fixture. If an existing closet lighting fixture juts out from the wall directly over the door or occupies any other area that could work more effectively as storage space, remove the lighting fixture and install it in a less obtrusive place.

Every corner of a closet should be illuminated. When things are in the dark, they get lost. Closet lighting should be as bright as possible. You shouldn't have to remove everything from the closet to find out if the blouse matches the skirt, or if there's really a spot on your pants.

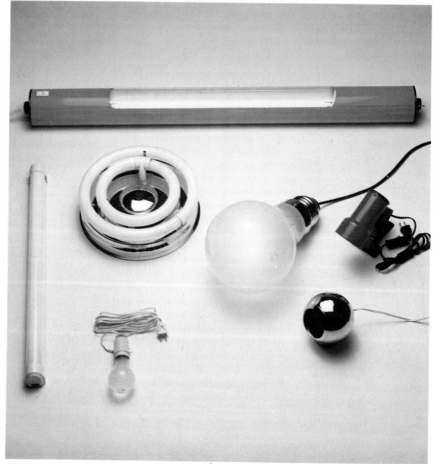

6. Snapit is equipped with wiring and a button that goes in the door frame so that the light goes on when the door opens and off when it shuts. (Cable Electric Products, Inc.)

7. Rotating wall-to-wall Wall Lamp spotlights a closet's contents not only from wall or ceiling, but from floor or shelf. (George Kovacs) Photo: Bruce Wolf

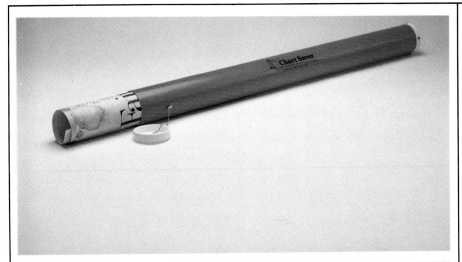

MAPPED OUT Nautical chart storage tube can hold leftover wrapping paper, posters and other outsize papers that normally collect dust propped on a closet's floor. The tube has a chain for hanging. (Goldbergs' Marine) Photo: Bruce Wolf

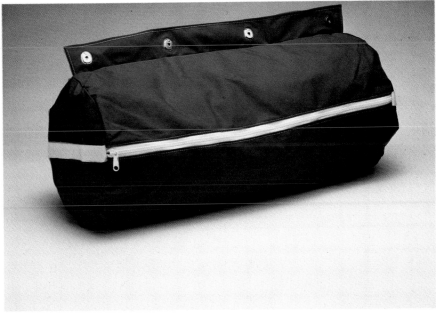

BULKED UP Canvas bulkhead stowage bag, designed for the wall of a yacht, comes in handy on closet walls, too—particularly in bathrooms or laundry rooms, since it's waterproof and the zipper is rustproof. (Goldbergs' Marine) Photo: Bruce Wolf

UP, UP AND AWAY Stowaway stepstool folds up to an inch in width and therefore can be stashed anywhere when it's not busy helping you get to your highest shelves. It has a handle on top for easy carrying—although many people avoid having to take it too far by having one per room. (Black and Decker) Photo: Bruce Wolf

SEA FARE

Boat designers are among the world's greatest storage experts. They have to be, for safety's sake. But a lot of their clever concepts are applicable on dry land, too, for making your closets shipshape.

REACHING THE HEIGHTS

There's no point in utilizing overhead space for storage if you have no means of reaching it. Any ladder will do, of course. But the ideal ladder is one that takes up only a wisp of space itself.

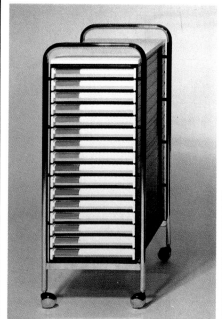

STRAIGHT AND NARROW The IDS System (the IDS Mobil is shown above) comes with compartmentalized drawers for documents, photo slides, hobby gear, art or writing supplies—virtually anything. (Menash)

MOD SQUAD Enameled steel Modular Storage Cabinets come in various colors and configurations, on casters or glides, in two widths—36 inch or 24 inch. Partitioned to hold slides, film canisters, cassettes, microfilm reels, video cassettes, filmloops, audio tapes, they can also hold jewelry and other accessories. (Bretford Manufacturing, Inc.)

FILING IN STYLE

Filing systems mean much more than the traditional big gray metal cabinet. There are file drawers shaped and partitioned just for tape cassettes, for instance, or for video cassettes, or for maps and other hard-to-store documents. These systems, which have organized many an office, film laboratory and graphic design studio, are equally useful for streamlining your closets at home—or since they're as good-looking as they are functional, for use as closet-furniture in any room.

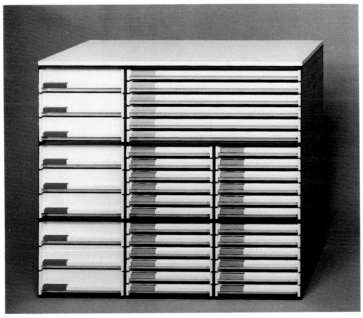

LONG-PLAYING STORAGE LP record storage module holds about 320 records in individual envelopes (or 300 records in their original jackets) per 36-inch cabinet. (Bretford Manufacturing, Inc.)

COLOR KEY Another version of the IDS System, the IDS Stabil, has color-coding on the drawers to help you remember what's where. (Menash)

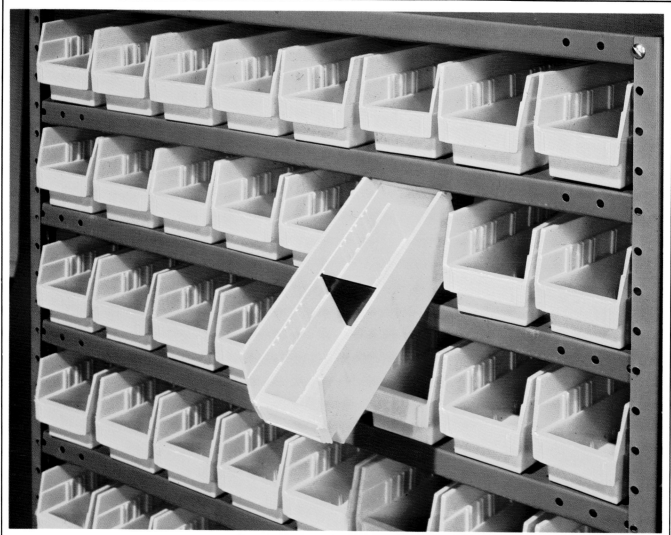

AKROBINS AkroBins can be fit into shelving for easy access. (Akro-Mils)

BOXES AND BINS

Industrial-parts storage systems came out of the factory with high-tech and into home closets (or elsewhere in homes). They proved so popular that many manufacturers are now producing lines especially for the home or marketing industrial units for home use, with great success. Small drawers and bins solve the perennial problem of where to stash tiny tools, art supplies, desk supplies—all the things that end up cluttering desk drawers or tabletops. Larger units help organize any item in

And while you're getting organized, don't overlook the potential of shelf dividers from the inventive world of commercial display, to give any shelf the neat look and efficiency you get with industrial bins.

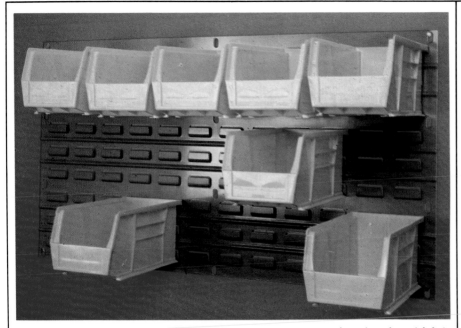

PRIMARY COLORS Versatile Akro-Bins can be hooked onto specially constructed metal units *(above)* or stacked on top of each other *(right)*. And they come in cheery colors for kids' rooms.

IT'S A STEEL Steel units designed for small parts storage in factories are equally efficient in homes. Cubbyhole sizes are adjustable. (Equipto)

UNDER COVER This under-counter box for retail stores is also handy on closet shelves. (Federal Fibre Corporation)

STAC-A-DRAWER One of Akro-Mils's numerous stacking drawer systems, they also come partitioned, transparent, encased in steel frames and made-to-fit into steel shelving.

TIDI-FILES The ideal solution for collections of magazines, comic books, old letters, memorabilia. Stash them on a shelf. (Frank Eastern Company)

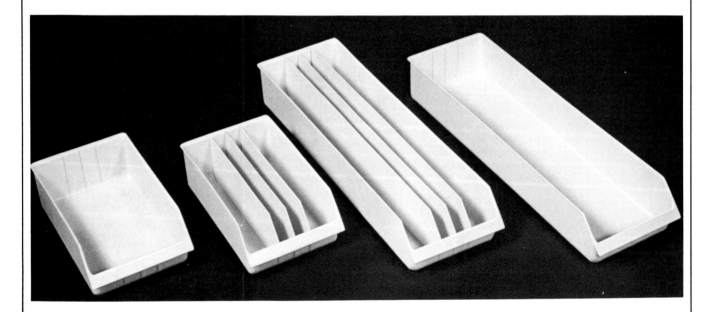

TOTELINE DRAWERS These are normally found in schools, laboratories and hospitals, but they're great shelf-dividers anywhere—easy to clean, available with or without dividers and lids. (Molded Fiber Glass Tray Company)

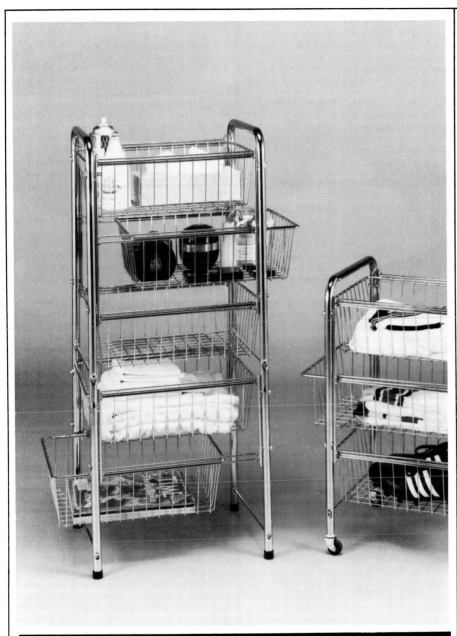

FURTHER ON BASKETS

The beauty of wire baskets is that they're as easily accessible as shelves—but unlike shelves, they help you categorize your belongings. Furthermore, baskets are see-through so you know at a glance what's in them. Put socks in one, underwear in another. Use them for pillowcases, sheets, towels, toys, handbags. Use them in any room of the house, in any closet, or—in the case of those that don't come on casters—on your shelves themselves!

CADDIES Hi-Rise Basket Caddy (*left*) contains chrome-plated basket drawers. It's 38 inches high, 13 inches wide and 16½ inches deep, and the Roll-A-Way Basket Caddy (*right*), 24 inches high, 13 inches wide and 16½ inches deep, sits on casters for mobility. Both are easily assembled. (Lee/Rowan)

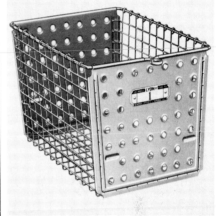

BASKET RACKS Like baskets usually found in locker rooms, the sides and bottoms of these are wire mesh; the fronts and backs are sheet steel. And with the (optional) number plates you can keep tabs on the baskets' contents. Units come with or without casters. (Lyon Metal Products, Inc.)

ELFA STORAGE BASKETS Elfa Basket/Drawers come in white or brown and are made of steel with heavy-duty epoxy finish. Depths range from flat to 15¼ inches. The baskets slide easily in and out on runner set-ups of various heights and widths, with or without casters. Elfa systems make more room in any room or closet. Or they can play basket-wall making two rooms out of one. (Federal Fibre Corporation)

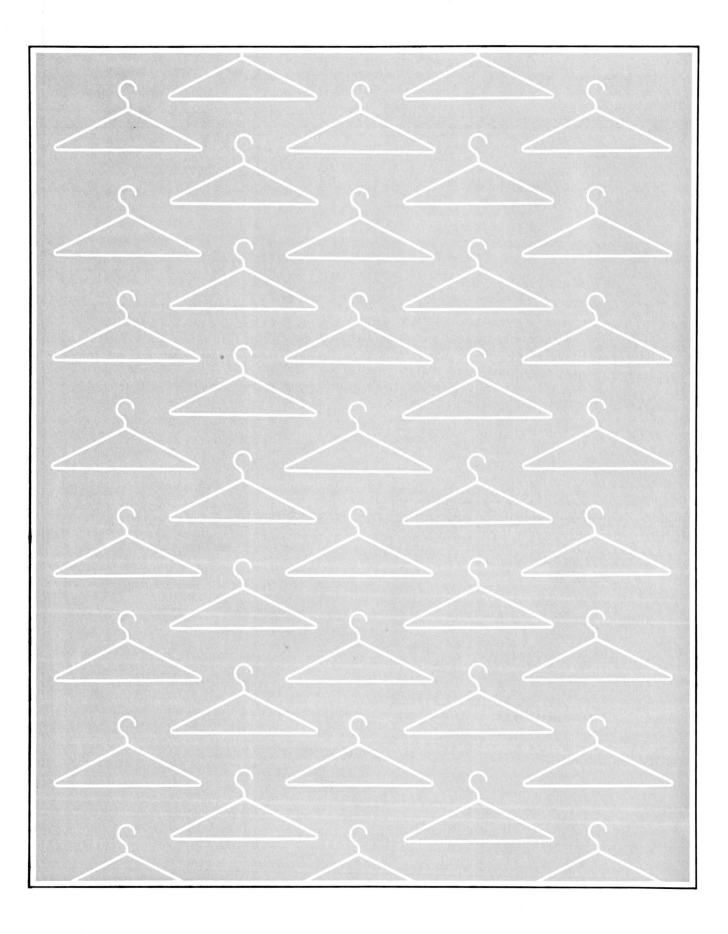

SOURCE GUIDE

Some manufacturers do not sell directly to consumers. However, if you write to them, most will refer you to a dealer in your area. Although many of the companies listed here offer myriad products, only those relevant to closets are mentioned.

Able Steel Equipment Co., Inc.
50-02 23 St.
Long Island City, NY 11101
Metal lockers and shelving

Adapto Steel Products
P.O. Box 1660
Hialeah, FL 33011
Metal lockers

Admac International
903 River Acres Dr.
Tecumseh, MI 49286
The Space Organizer

Akro-Mils
Box 989
Akron, OH 44309
Bins, stacking drawers

Allibert, Inc.
182 Madison Ave.
New York, NY 10016
Bathroom accessories

Architectural Supplements, Inc.
341A East 62 St.
New York, NY 10021
Hooks, knobs

Atelier International, Ltd.
595 Madison Ave.
New York, NY 10022
Furniture

Beacon Enterprises, Inc.
230 Fifth Ave.
New York, NY 10001
Shoe racks

Bevco Precision Manufacturing Co.
831 Chicago Ave.
Evanston, IL 60202
Luggage stands, hangers

Beylerian Ltd.
225 Fifth Ave.
New York, NY 10010
Furniture, storage systems

Black and Decker, Inc.
Towson, MD 21204
Folding ladders

Bloomingdale's
1000 Third Ave.
New York, NY 10022
Hangers, accessories

Bretford Manufacturing, Inc.
9715 Soreng Ave.
Schiller Park, IL 60176
Video storage systems

Cable Electric Products
P.O. Box 6767
Providence, RI 02940
Lighting

Caswell-Massey Co., Ltd.
575 Lexington Ave.
New York, NY 10022
Sachets, potpourris

Claridge Products
  and Equipment, Inc.
P.O. Box 910
Harrison, AR 72601
Classroom storage systems

Closet King
430 East 72 St.
New York, NY 10021
Accessories, closet furnishings

Closet Maid Corp.
720 Southwest 17 St.
Ocala, FL 32670
*Plastic-coated closet systems and
  shelving*

Closet Spacesaver Co.
180 West 58 St.
New York, NY 10019
Closet systems

Columbia Lighting Inc.
North 3808 Sullivan Rd.
Box 2787
Spokane, WA 99220
Lighting

Conran's
160 E. 54 St.
New York, NY 10022
Furniture

Designworks, Ltd.
27 E. 67 St.
New York, NY 10021
Hangers

Designers Guild
277 Kings Rd.
London SW3 England
Sachets

Elfa Division
Swedish Wire Products, Inc.
P.O. Box 861
1755 A Wilwat Dr.
Norcross, GA 30091
Elfa basket storage systems

Henry A. Enrich & Co., Inc.
350 Fifth Ave.
New York, NY 10001
Garment bags, closet software

Equipto
225 S. Highland Ave.
Aurora, IL 60507
Containers, accessories

Federal Fibre Corp.
P.O. Box 395
Bellmawr, NJ 08031
Boxes and containers

Frank Eastern Co.
625 Broadway
New York, NY 10012
*Office furnishings, steel shelf units,
  special files*

Garcy Corp
491-B Edward H. Ross Dr.
Elmwood Park, NJ 07407
Metal track systems

General Electric
Cleveland, OH 44112
Lighting

Goldbergs' Marine
202 Market St.
Philadelphia, PA 19106
Marine supplies

Grayline Housewares
1616 Berkley St.
Elgin, IL 60120
*Plastic coated space-saving
  accessories*

Gries Reproducer Co.
Div. of Coats & Clark
New Rochelle, NY 10902
Small hooks

Hammacher Schlemmer
147 E. 57 St.
New York, NY 10022
Accessories and closet furnishings

Hammer-Pac, Inc.
350 Fifth Ave.
New York, NY 10001
The Hooker

Hastings Tile & Il Bagno Collection
964 Third Ave.
New York, NY 10022
Bath furnishings, storage furniture,
Poggenpohl

Heller Designs, Inc.
41 Madison Ave.
New York, NY 10010
Record racks, grids

IDG Marketing Ltd.
1100 Slocum Ave.
Ridgefield, NJ 07657
Hooks

Interlake Inc.
135 St. and Perry Ave.
Chicago, IL 60627
Storage bins and systems

Interlubke
International Contract
    Furnishings, Inc.
145 E. 57 St.
New York, NY 10022
Closet wall systems

IPC Inc.
5th & Mitchell Sts.
Lansdale, PA 19446
The ultimate (swivel) hanger

Iron-A-Way Inc.
220 W. Jackson
Morton, IL 61550
Built-in ironing boards

Knape & Vogt Manufacturing Co.
2700 Oak Industrial Dr., N.E.
Grand Rapids, MI 49505
Hardware

George Kovacs Lighting, Inc.
24 W. 40 St.
New York, NY 10018
Lighting

Landes
P.O. Box 2197
Gardena, CA 90247
Wood "closet furniture," Northridge
Collection

Lee/Rowan
6333 Etzel Ave.
St. Louis, MO 63133
Closet accessories

Lewis of London
215 E. 51 St.
New York, NY 10022
Children's furniture

l'Herbier de Provence
156 E. 64 St.
New York, NY 10021
Sachets, potpourris

Lyon Metal Products, Inc.
P.O. Box 671
Aurora, IL 60507
Baskets

Meilink Safe Co.
6245 Industrial Parkway
Box 2458
Whitehouse, OH 43571
Safes

Menash
2305 Broadway
New York, NY 10024
File systems for documents, video
gear, hobby gear, art supplies, etc.

Metropolitan Wire Corp.
Wilkes-Barre, PA 18705
Metal baskets, shelf systems

Molded Fiber Glass Tray Co.
East Erie St.
Linesville, PA 16424
Boxes

Mutschler
302 S. Madison St.
Nappanee, IN 46550
Kitchen cabinetry

NesTier
Midland-Ross Corp.
10605 Chester Rd.
Cincinnati, OH 45215
Boxes

Pappagallo
1250 Broadway
New York, NY 10001
Shoe bags

Peter Pepper
17929 S. Susana Rd.
Compton, CA 90221
Hooks, knobs

Railex Corporation
89-02 Atlantic Ave.
Queens, NY 11416
Automated conveyor systems

Reefer-Galler
4044 Park Ave.
St. Louis, MO 63110
Antimoth sachets and sprays

Reston Lloyd, Ltd.
P.O. Box 2302
Reston, VA 22090
Plastic accessories

Rubbermaid Inc.
1147 Akron Rd.
Wooster, OH 44691
Bathroom and kitchen organizers

Scandinavian Design, Inc.
127 E. 59 St.
New York, NY 10022
Wall closet systems

Schulte Corporation
11450 Grooms Rd.
Cincinnati, OH 45242
Sani-Shelf ventilated shelving

Sherle Wagner
60 E. 57 St.
New York, NY 10022
Hooks, bathroom accessories

Sid Diamond
379 Fifth Ave.
New York, NY 10016
Display systems

Stay-Neat
132 Division St.
Boonton, NJ 07005
Closet systems

Sun Glo Corp.
Box 348
Chappaqua, NY 10514
Wood shelving units

Joseph Teklits Woodcraft Corp.
345 E. 104 St.
New York, NY 10029
Carpentry

Up & Co.
190 Hubbell St.
San Francisco, CA 94107
Freestanding, portable closets

Vogel-Peterson Co.
Rte. 83 & Madison St.
Elmhurst, IL 60126
Coat racks, hangers and hooks

White Machine Co., Inc.
50 Boright Ave.
Kenilworth, NJ 07033
Automated conveyor systems

Whitmor Manufacturing Co., Inc.
350 Fifth Ave.
New York, NY 10001
Garment and accessory bags

INDEX